CLEO

IRISH CLOTHES IN A WIDER WORLD

Hilary O'Kelly

Æ
ASSOCIATED EDITIONS

To Kitty Joyce, and to all who have made and sustained Cleo

Cleo: Irish Clothes in a Wider World
Published in January 2014 by Associated Editions,
33 Melrose Avenue, Fairview, Dublin 3, Ireland
www.associatededitions.ie

Photography, unless stated, from Cleo archive and by William Gallagher or Marta Bustillo.

Every effort has been made by the author to acknowledge correct copyright of images where applicable. Any errors or omissions are unintentional.

Book design by VERMILLON

A CIP record for this title is available from the British Library

ISBN 978-1-906429-21-8

Acknowledgements

In researching this history of Cleo I have had generous assistance from many people, to all of whom I am very grateful.

First and foremost I wish to thank Kitty Joyce who gave her time and energy to the project. She approached my endeavour as she does her own, with focus, matched by an inclination for adventure. I would also like to thank the Joyce family for their help, Tom Joyce, Bryan, Mary, Mark, Helen, Stephen and Sarah Joyce.

The publication of this research was generously facilitated by The Golden Fleece Award, established by the late Lillias Mitchell. I am very grateful to the Trustees for their support of the project while still a proposal, and their constancy to its publication.

Thanks also to the estate of Bill Doyle, in the care of his daughter Leslie Doyle.

Many friends, family, colleagues and people I have never met, kindly shared their experience and responses to Cleo, while others provided helpful images, texts, references, advice and introductions. For contributions of every kind I would like to thank:

James Arnold; Jaclyn Bashoff; Jane Behan; Eugenia Bell; Ben Bonaldi; Anne Brady; Knut Bry and Tinagent.com; Betty Byrne; Fiona Byrne; Garech Browne; Róisín de Buitléir; Mike Bunn; Marta Bustillo; Linda Byrne; Paul Caffrey; Liz Clery; Finbarr Connolly; Rose Mary Craig; Úna Crowe; Margaret Cullen; Clare Daly; Annie Dibble; Willie Donnelly; Clodagh Doyle; Rose Doyle; Clare Drury; Catherine Drury; John Dunavant; Kevin Dunne; Sarah Durcan; Paul Durcan; Tony Farmar; Nuala Fenton; Sarah Finlay; Josephine Gallagher; William Gallagher; Frances Gillespie; Lisa Godson; Nicola Gordon Bowe; Sheila Gorman; Niamh Harte; Elaine Hewitt; Betty Hewitt; Éamonn Hurley; Anjelica Huston; Kieran Johnson and staff at The Richard Avedon Foundation; Noirin Kennedy Pye; Maureen Lewis; Cliodhna Mahon; Carol Mantle; Millie Mantle; Éadaoin Marrinan; Catherine Martin; James Martin; Edward Murphy; Neil McCullough; Catherine Michel; The nieces and extended family of Lillias Mitchell; My own beloved nieces; Michael Molloy; Beth Moran; Geraldine O'Doherty; Maria O'Donovan; Ann O'Kelly; Anne O'Kelly; Breffnie O'Kelly; Brendan O'Kelly; Brian O'Kelly; Colette O'Kelly. Kevin O'Kelly; Paul O'Kelly; Conor O'Riordan; Helen Rock; Alice Roden; Donna Romano; Anne Roper; Veronica Rowe; Ellen Rowley; Vera Ryan; William J. Smyth; Bob Sower; Neasa Travers; Joanne Turney; Betty Wall; Alex Ward; Staff at The J. Peterman Company; Staff of the Irish Architectural Archive; Staff of the National Library, Staff of the National Photographic Archive, Colleagues in National College of Art & Design (NCAD); particularly staff of the Edward Murphy Library and staff of National Irish Visual Arts Library, NCAD; Visual Resources, NCAD.

And finally there are many others, unmentioned here, to whom I hope to convey my sincere thanks in person.

In 2012 Kitty Joyce donated the Cleo archive to the National Irish Visual Arts library (NIVAL) at the National College of Art & Design (NCAD) 100 Thomas Street, Dublin 8.

Contents

. . .

Such as the woman passer-by who stopped me on Duke Street:

"You don't know me but I knew your father!

. . .

I am 82 and I am as new as a snowdrop.

No, not a snowdrop, a sunflower.

I've just been looking in the window of CLEO'S in Kildare Street.

Do you know it? She sells Celtic Clothes. A gem of a shop.

She's got a vase of sunflowers in the middle of the window

And, all around it, garments

Of every hue of gold you have ever seen,

Every lunula, every monstrance.

It could be an altar in St Petersburg, CLEO'S window,

An iconic boutique, all hand-knitted vestments,

The holiness of the soul's body, no less!

I said to myself: This is ME, this window!

This window is ME!

CLEO'S is ME!

...

Paul Durcan

Excerpt from *The Recession* (lines 6-7 and 20-33)

From the collection *Praise in Which I live and Work and Have My Being* (2012)
Published by Harvill Secker, London.
With kind permission of Paul Durcan.

A selection of Cleo sweaters, hand-knit in myriad stitches and patterns, from a palette of coloured wools sent by Kitty Joyce to the knitters. While the diverse rhythms and tensions reflect the various hands that made them, their very proficiency almost belies the domestic, hand-crafted origin (characteristic of more amateur work, like that illustrated on p. 34).

A CLEO VIEW

CLEO, Irish Clothes in a Wider World

Cleo is among the oldest surviving family-run shops in the heart of Dublin, for the best part of a century commissioning and selling work that encapsulates the image of Ireland at home and abroad – hand knits and hand weaves. And yet, among most Irish people, it barely registers. In fact, Cleo customers are, for the most part, more used to shopping in New York, Paris, London or Tokyo. Their enthusiasm, even love, for what they find in the Georgian house at 18 Kildare Street can come as a surprise to those who have passed it casually all their lives. For many visitors it is a highlight of, if not the reason for, visiting Dublin; some leave the shop laden down with colourful wool and linen clothes while others emerge with just a single garment.

It may well be the very familiarity of knitting and weaving that render them invisible to many at home. But visitors hoping to encounter something particular and special to Ireland feel they have found it when they visit Cleo. Some regard the shop as a place lost in time, unchanged for decades. But, as an independent, living business Cleo is constantly changing, to its own quiet rhythm, and with a keen awareness of the wider world.

This history of Cleo started from conversation with its owner Kitty Joyce (the source of all unreferenced quotations) and developed through examining order books, sample books, customer correspondence and articles surviving from the mid 1950s. Earlier records were, sadly, discarded through lack of space when the shop moved in the 1970s. Although the focus is on Cleo, the account offers a vignette of business and life in Ireland over much of the 20th century.

Almost thirty years before the government-commissioned 'Scandinavian Report' advocated guarding and promoting local craft as the future for *Design in Ireland* (1962), Cleo was bringing together Irish materials, local skills and international customers. Almost forty years before T.K. Whittaker published his pivotal *The First Programme for Economic Expansion* (1958), advocating the dismantling of protectionist policies in favour of international markets for our

cleo's SPECIALISE IN CLOTHES MADE FROM NATURAL FIBRES - WOOL AND LINEN, OF IRISH ORIGIN.
WE CHOOSE OUR FABRICS FOR THEIR BEAUTY, QUALITY AND TEXTURE.
MANY OF OUR DESIGNS ARE DRAWN FROM IRELAND'S PAST.
" WEARABLE ART " TO TREASURE AND HAND ON.CLEO'S IS A COMPANY WORKED BY THREE GENERATIONS OF THE JOYCE FAMILY, FROM 1936 TO THE PRESENT.

Cleo, in their own words. From their promitional brochure, c. 1993.

produce, Mrs Ryan of Cleo had been sending Irish goods across the globe. Today, Cleo remains equally ahead of its time by dealing in local, sustainable and fair trade practices, perspectives only recently forming in the public consciousness.

Cleo is a business dealing in hand knit sweaters and Irish weaving. As a traditional practice passed on unbroken from generation to generation in Ireland, since at least the Famine, hand knitting is actually a rarity. The work has long been associated particularly with women, and with the home, because, it has been suggested, it is consistent with a reliance on women for child rearing.[1] Not requiring rapt attention – unlike, say, machine harvesting, or smelting - it allows an eye to be kept on the children while working, and in a crisis the work can be dropped without grave danger to persons or production. Both knitting and weaving are skills for which Ireland has an international reputation, earned not only through their inherent qualities but also through their worldwide promotion.

That knitwear and sweaters remain central to the popular Irish image of warmth and home is again underlined by their prominence in advertising for 'The Gathering', Fáilte Ireland's initiative encouraging family, friends and emigrants to visit Ireland in 2013. To promote this outreach festival, invitation postcards were distributed to households countrywide, picturing the 'welcome home' message with a cheery gathering, fronted by a trio clad in patterned knit sweaters, in the colours of the national flag.

On the related website the sweaters are linked with the exhortation 'create' which, apart from signalling the spontaneous sociability of Ireland, helps suggest an atmosphere supportive of the imagination associated with knitwear. These particular sweaters, however, appear machine-knit, lack the personality or individuality of the handmade original, and their apparent manufacture in fibre mixes may offer indeed less of the warmth.

Integral to this account of Cleo is how, at an official level, knitting skills (along with perhaps other crafts in Ireland) while often lauded, have been valued less in their own right than as means to a commercial, industrial or even ideological end. Quality knitting has instead been privately sustained in homes and in small enterprise. In Cleo the craft has been nurtured as much for its creative and social value, Kitty Joyce's response to this collective inheritance stemming from an artistic sensibility as well as a business sense. Rather than regarding what she sells as 'product' from 'suppliers' she sees it as the work of 'gifted makers'. Her own role she considers not as 'a job' but as 'work' to be of value in people's lives.

This Cleo vision, and sense of responsibility within society, having woven a way through varied paths over 80 years, has now found itself coinciding with today's leading design thinking.[2] Cleo's practice relies on a relationship of trust between maker and seller, a dynamic now important in sustainable thinking just as much as values of considered consumption, careful disposal and product recycling.

The polymath Richard Sennett, a leading analyst of the nature of society within cities and urban structures, asserts in *The Craftsman* (2008) that society needs craftwork as a way to keep people rooted in material reality. From his investigations of cities, labour and culture, Sennett has concluded the desire to do a job well for its own sake is a basic human impulse, and that craft provides

Fáilte Ireland's invitation postcard to 'the gathering', 2013. (By kind permission of The Gathering).

a steadying balance in a world which overrates intellectual prowess. Similarly, David Gauntlet in 'Making is Connecting' (2011) suggests the importance of the process of making as a means of forming connections: between abstract ideas and physical materials, between one person and another, and between individuals and their place in society through a deeper sense of embededdness and participation in the world.

. . .

A parallel philosophy has been developed in Cleo over many years, in their grounded attitude to materials, style, making and trade. The connections and social geography woven into Cleo's history embrace complex relationships across borders, status and cultures. The story involves of course many people, but at the centre are Kitty Joyce and her mother Kit Ryan, on whom the account focuses. Important too is the culture of wool, its capacities and reputation, connecting rural Ireland and Dublin with an international and sometimes more glamorous world beyond. Cleo's position as a crossroads between country Ireland and the cosmopolitan is brought to life in a recollection of Mike Bunn, the celebrated photographer of Irish fashion. As he enjoyed a home-cooked lunch there (prepared daily in Cleo) 'an attractive French woman dashed in on her way from The Shelbourne to the airport. She tried on a pair of fisherman's trousers, a sweater and a crios belt and left the shop - with her own clothes in the Cleo bag.' She looked so well, he said, 'she would stop the plane.' His account neatly takes in the blend of the homely and the air age that have characterised Cleo since it, and Aer Lingus, were founded in the same year almost 80 years ago.

Cleo was established in 1936, by Kit Ryan, mother of the current proprietor Kitty Joyce. She built her business despite the gloom of the 1930s and '40s and saw it flourish in the early years of airline tourism from the U.S.A. in the 1950s and '60s. Through the 1970s Cleo survived inflation, strikes, material shortages and political instability mainly by concentrating on export to America. When this American trade dipped in the 1980s, Europe and Japan were cultivated as more significant markets, if not quite replacements for the U.S. As the economy straitened further Cleo, rather than retreat, expanded, first by opening a new

Cleo, 2 Shelbourne Street, Kenmare, Co. Kerry is located, like Cleo Dublin, in a well-appointed town house retaining its original domestic scale and layout.

shop in Kenmare in 1985, and by experimenting with other outlets in Ireland and with franchises abroad. While two of Kitty's daughters work directly with Cleo, Helen in Kenmare and Sarah in Dublin, the shop is inevitably part of the lives of all her six children, and of Kitty's farming husband, Tom Joyce.

From the early days Cleo's founder, Mrs Ryan, bridged a divide between bespoke and readymade clothing, offering quality garments that were of the highest standard without being the latest fashions. As a result, they can often appear (when indeed they are noticed) to the domestic buyer as 'very expensive', but in fact Cleo prices have always been comparable to quality garments for sale in nearby department stores. In stark contrast with the contemporary retail environment, Cleo continues to offer an individual local product, with personalised service, in a central location. This is increasingly rare in Dublin, where rents preclude almost all but global chains from operating in prime locations. In Ireland's capital today, therefore, worldwide branded clothes predominate in shops styled uniformly as they are across the developed world. Their homogeneity is achieved within a global network; fabrics and clothing, designed in one location, made in another - perhaps thousands of miles away - decorated somewhere else, then packaged, branded and distributed across the planet, to appear in plate-glassed window displays, again styled according to an international manual dictating the layout and merchandising of the outlet. Short term shop-staff are taught to push 'the latest' goods but less about their materials, making or care.

In this mainstream retail arena, shop entrances have become wide open portals minimising the transition from street to sales floor, easing customers across the threshold to browse racks of clothes, all strategically merchandised to encourage multiple purchases. Each garment is bar-coded and electronically tagged to trigger an alarm if illicitly taken. Mechanised stock control, backed up by burly security staff, allows the bigger store convey a carefree attitude to its commodified stock, and reduces, but does not prevent, shop-lifting, the cost of which is factored into retail prices. By contrast, going into Cleo on Kildare Street has a ceremonial dimension; no customer simply 'drifts' in. After climbing a few stone steps, the hall door, always ajar during business hours, gives access to an inner door, with a door bell, that is opened for each customer. In quieter Kenmare Cleo's door is always simply open.

The divergence between smaller specialist providers and larger department and chain stores accelerated with the globalisation of much 20th century trade. But in the 21st century the local, individual and sustainable appear set to play a bigger part, and some idea of a shared future might be possible through exploring the past of this one shop. Cleo trades mainly in hand knitting and weaving. The long history in Ireland of both can prompt the perception of them as merely historic practices producing old fashioned, 'heritage' products. However, Cleo's history would rather suggest that hand knitting and weaving have survived through versatility and adaptation to changing tastes and fluctuating social and economic conditions. The very adaptability of plain and purl stitches, knit by hand or machine, can result in an Aran sweater or Calvin Klein underwear. A warp and weft can produce a *crios* belt or an industrial fan belt.

Despite this innate versatility and adaptability, an aura of nostalgia persists around Irish knitting, based on its rural associations and the domestic setting for much of its production. It is among the best surviving craft skills in the country. Yet, the practice of hand knitting seems to fall outside the realm of 'traditional craft' not on account of any marginal status - but on the contrary - because of its integration into everyday life. Again, in *The Craftsman*, Richard Sennett proposes considering:

> what the process of making concrete things reveals to us about ourselves. Learning from things requires us to care about the qualities of cloth or the right way to poach fish; fine cloth or food cooked well enables us to imagine larger categories of "good"... I want to make the case... that people can learn about themselves through the things they make, that material culture matters.[3]

Hand knitting, currently enjoying another fashionable renaissance, has for decades been routinely overlooked and even disparaged, posited as an unthinking occupation of limited worth. In discussing the nature and value of craft, for example, the influential and prolific *Irish Times* journalist, Fintan O'Toole, acting as conference moderator, addressed The World Crafts Council gathering in Dublin in 2011, sketching two extremities of craft straddling the banal to the sublime:

Two Irish sweaters; one from Cleo (left) is densly knit with Irish wool in complex stitches and will hold its shape and warmth for decades. The other, more loosely knit in softer wool, is likely to loose shape more quickly, although it cost more than the Cleo sweater by $10 ($120 versus $110). The less intricate work, however, has been increasingly manufactured as being more appropriate to modern requirements for faster manufacture, lower production costs and suitability to modern consumption in warmer houses. Perhaps rising fuel costs and a renewed appreciation for longevity in garments may result in a revision of these ideas. (Photographed for *GQ* 1981. Copyright Knut Bry represented by Tinagent.com).

> perhaps the usefulness of the idea of craft lies in its very fuzziness. It covers a vast range of phenomena ... from knitting a jumper while watching *The Late Late Show* to producing objects of heart-stopping beauty.[4]

From this perspective it would appear the jumper itself would never be an object of heart-stopping beauty. It is not a view shared by Cleo, who have nurtured individual and small-scale makers and consumers for quality Irish textiles, helping sustain Ireland's international reputation for wool and linen achieved since at least the 15th century.[5] Since that period, despite numerous and varied assaults on the industry, and the vicissitudes of political and economic interference over many centuries, the reputation for Irish wool and linen endures into the 21st century.

The high standing of Irish textiles has been achieved abroad, not only by virtue of their intrinsic quality, but via trade and business and also the support of promotional work by philanthropists, of whom Lady Aberdeen, at the end of the 19th century, is the most renowned.[6] Irish linen, Irish lace, Irish tweeds and Irish wool have consequently been part of many international wardrobes and households for over a hundred, if not hundreds, of years. Anyone with an interest in cloth and craft hope to see this heritage when they visit Ireland. Others with emotional ties to the country hope to find a warm reminder of their visit and this often takes the shape of a woolen garment or blanket. But where does a visitor find such a thing? Most craft and tourist shops do not offer real hand-knitting or quality hand-made textiles. A discerning customer can distinguish hand-knitting made with skill and imagination from the machine knit, or even computer-generated work, available in more popular gift shops, often not even made in Ireland.

Encouraging shoppers, Irish as well as foreign, to buy Irish products has been attempted by local business and nationalist causes for centuries but not always with great success. The new Free State government continued the efforts in the 1930s when:

> Self sufficiency was a key Fianna Fáil objective, close to De Valera's heart because it represented a rejection of the modern world. In 1933 he urged the women of Ireland to turn their backs on the fashions of Paris, London and New York, dressing only in Irish tweeds and woolens until Irish cottons and silks became available. However Irish consumers were less inclined to reject modern consumerism than De Valera might have wished.[7]

It is interesting that businesses established either in the aftermath of the Famine, under the Congested Districts Board, or under the Free State government, have remained until now arguably the backbone of Irish cloth and clothing. Of these, for example, Magees of Donegal was established in 1866, The Woollen Mills on the Dublin quays in 1888 and Kennedy & McSharry in 1890. Under the Free State government, in 1928, Dwyers of Cork, who wholesaled clothes to draperies in every town and village throughout 20th century Ireland, was established. In 1936 Cleo opened, as did men's outfitters Kevin & Howlin. And in 1940 Murphy Sheehy, now at the heart of home dress-making in Ireland, was set up as import substitution became policy – selling Irish sheets and blankets to the trade, in place of imported stock. In the 1970s, as it moved into dress and furnishing fabric, Murphy Sheehy sourced end-of-line cloth from the surrounding rag-trade manufacturers. As that skilled trade began to move out of the city, and later out of Ireland, their business developed, sourcing bolts of fabric from woollen mills and small scale manufacturers who were closing down.[8]

De Valera's advocating of Irish cloth in place of foreign fashions is easily characterised as promoting dowdiness over style, strengthening a common perception of Irishness as anti-fashion and anti-modern. It also served to link an introverted nationalism with Irish cloth and clothing. On the other hand, Irish tweeds and lace had long been promoted by the Anglo-Irish and Ascendancy, through exhibitions and demonstrations, framing the crafts for middle-class consumption.[9] Thus a taste for Irish produce had conversely also become characteristic of their set. The latest and best remembered of these enterprises was the much loved Country Shop, which survived from 1930 until 1978 at 23 St Stephen's Green. Established by Muriel Gahan, Olivia Hughes, Paddy Somerville -Large, Lucy Franks and Vida Lentaigne, from the beginning The Country Shop had a distinct mission and set of objectives, overseen by a board of directors:

1. To help the people in the poor districts in the west by encouraging and supporting home industries such as hand spinning, weaving and knitting.
2. To encourage individual craftworkers such as smiths and carpenters in the country, and all other country industries and country products.
3. To promote and assist the work of the United Irishwomen in the country.[10]

This undoubted idealism may also have reflected an element of paternalism towards the crafts being fostered, as suggested in the remarks of EF Sutton, first chairman of The Crafts Council of Ireland:

> Dr Gahan, in reference to the homespuns, and in particular to the innate skill of the weavers commented recently that: " The weavers didn't realise the beauty of what they were doing – they did it from poverty and necessity." She knew them and worked with them.[11]

Such dual support for for Irish cloth and clothing, then, can be seen to make conflicting cultural declarations; entrenched nationalism or privileged beneficence. A popular perception in Ireland is consequently of tweeds and handknits being Anglo-Irish, or alternatively what may be characterised as 'Bean Uí Báinín'. This apparent paradox is identified by Declan Kiberd in the work of Republican playwright Brendan Behan, where 'the seeming opposite becomes an actual double.... If the warders in *The Quare Fellow* were finally indistinguishable from the prisoners, so in *The Hostage* kilted rebels are intistinguishable from

moustachioed colonels.'[12] Cleo, however, grows out of neither de Valeran nor Anglo-Irish ideology. More than either, it enfranchises the creativity of the individual maker, rooting in a practical sense a Ruskinian vision of democratic vernacular forms. Less instructively conceived, it is a hands-on enterprise based on a real business drive focusing on local skills, attention to detail and intuition.

As a craft enterprise dealing in clothing, Cleo falls outside easy categorisation, and thus the clear remit of any particular promotional body. Though not fashion, it is clothing, and though clothing it is craft. Despite this difficulty in 'defining' Cleo and despite the many and varied manifestations of tweed and wool, one response appears constant in visual, literary, political and popular discourse; the opposition of knitting and tweed to 'modernity' remains persistent. Cleo's clientele and merchandise over seventy years, however, would suggest the possibility of alternative readings. As Tanya Harrod shows in relation to the inter-war years (noting it may be a more frequently recurring paradox) 'an important part of being modern was to be anti-modern.'[13] The history of Cleo certainly suggests that tradition and modernity, often seen in opposition, in reality co-exist in an evolving dialogue.

Endnotes

1 Hemmings, Jessica (2012) *The Textile Reader*, London, New York Berg, pp 321-323. Excerpt from Elizabeth Wayland Barber (1994) *Women's Work: The First 20,000 Years: Women, Cloth, and Society in Early Times* (1994) Oxford, Berg.

2 See for example the work of John Thackara (2005) *In The Bubble: Designing in a Complex World*, Cambridge, Mass., MIT Press.

3 Sennett, Richard (2008) *The Craftsman*, London, Penguin, p.8.

4 See also *The Irish Times* (11 June 2011) 'Art's less glamorous sister has been slaving away for decades' p. 9.

5 The standard reference for early Irish dress and textiles is Mairead Dunlevy (1989) *Dress in Ireland*, London, Batsford.

6 See Helland, Janice (2007) *British and Irish Home Arts and Industries 1880-1914: Marketing Craft, Making Fashion*, Dublin and Portland, Irish Academic Press. Also O'Kelly, Hilary (1992) 'Reconstructing Irishness' in *Chic Thrills*, Eds. Juliet Ash and Elizabeth Wilson, London, Pandora, pp. 75–82.

7 Daly, Mary E. (1992) *Industrial Development and Irish National Identity, 1922-1939*, Dublin, Gill and Macmillan, p. 90.

8 See Hopkin, Arlene (2007) *Murphy Sheehy: The biggest little treasure trove*, unpublished thesis NCAD.

9 For further discussion on a similar theme relating to USA see: Adamson, Glenn (2007) *Thinking Through Craft*, Oxford, New York, Berg p.112.

10 Mitchell, Geraldine (1997) *Deeds Not Words, The Life and Work of Muriel Gahan*, Dublin, Town House, p. 73.

11 Sutton, E.F. (1980) *Weaving: The Irish Inheritance*, Dublin, Gilbert Dalton, p. 44.

12 Kiberd, Declan (1995) *Inventing Ireland: The Literature of The Modern Nation*, London, Jonathan Cape, p. 526.

13 Harrod, Tanya (1999) *The Crafts in Britain in the 20th Century*, New Haven and London, Yale, p. 145.

10 SOUTH ANNE STREET

From Gowns to Handknits

"It'll be all the same in a hundred years" is Grafton Street's motto... for she keeps on finding that men and women remain the same, with life's seduction just as sweet to them, however the years recede with their fashions and fanaticisms...In a country that is never done boasting about its saints and doctors, where martyrs are three a penny and crucifixes bleed and statues bow to parishioners as if the 18th century had never been...where mists are the back-cloth and lamentations are the orchestra... Grafton Street still slithers easily from Stephen's Green to College Green...and remains...the unchallenged principal street, a persistent and contradictory piece of Ireland's self-expression.

Kate O'Brien, *Without My Cloak*, 1931[1]

DUBLIN & DRESS

When Cleo was established in Dublin in 1936, the clothing requirements of the city were catered for by department stores, drapers, tailors, dressmakers and the second hand trade as well as suppliers of fabrics, yarns and accessories.[2] Clothiers existed in great abundance - but by comparison with today, people owned very few clothes and what they had they mostly valued and looked after. Readymade clothes were largely imported from Britain although by the 1930s official policy aimed, through tariffs and import substitution, to replace this with local production.[3] Much Irish clothing was still hand made or homemade however, and in this process, acquiring new clothes required considerable commitment on the part of the person to be dressed. In the process of hand making, each individual garment was conceived from a bolt of cloth, which meant the customer was more deeply invested in the creativity of getting dressed. With paper dress patterns not yet as established as they later became, each design involved a discussion between maker and wearer. These discussions were followed by dress-fittings to check the progress and fit of the garment, and to allow an opportunity of adapting to unforeseen problems such as an unsuccessful design or a shortage of cloth. And then, just when you hoped to wear your new garment, it regularly took several visits to the maker; only to find it still was not ready for collection.[4]

A widespread conception of early 20th century Ireland is that of a poorly dressed people beyond the reaches of fashion, but the photographic evidence often suggests otherwise. At least on high days, holidays or simply going outside the immediate environment of home, most people, except the poorest, could rise to a 'rig-out' decent enough to pass themselves as respectable - even if it meant they had to beg, borrow or steal the clothes. Before the 1960s ushered in values of youthful, casual and transient style, a respectable established appearance was defined by tailoring, grooming and grown-up formality. Anybody aspiring to a

SMITHS
SMITHS
WE

modicum of social status dressed up going into town. In Dublin the area around Grafton Street was then, as now, the centre of the city's elite shopping district. This profile, today maintained through high commercial rents and retail prices, was then reinforced by a more hands-on physical management of the public space. Although a prestigious 'enclave', Grafton Street was not far from inner city housing where children would play out on the streets or nearby in St Stephen's Green. But should any unkempt youngsters wander onto Grafton Street they would quickly be sent packing by the police for fear of 'lowering the tone' of the area.[5]

The prevalence of businesses dealing in the necessaries of self-presentation is confirmed by Dublin business records. Before the arrival of chain stores offering entire 'looks', it took an extensive range of specialist traders to serve the clothing and grooming needs of the city. To take South Anne Street for example, where Cleo was first located, a person could be respectably turned out from top to toe on this one street alone, by the small Irish businesses trading in mantles, gowns, millinery, shoes, coiffure and luggage.

Walking from Grafton Street to Dawson Street on the left hand side of South Anne Street, the first shop was Vard furriers. Vard still trades on South Anne Street but in smaller premises, reflecting a change in attitudes to fur from a time when so many fashionable women were draped - at least in a single fox. Next door was a boot and shoemaker, Mr John Ryan. An arts and crafts shop occupied no 3 and Margaret McClure, hairdresser no 4. Weirs textile manufacturer and agent was in no 8, - and as today Keogh's pub was on the corner at Duke Lane. Across the small intersection was no 10 South Anne Street, where Cleo shared what Kitty recalls as a handsome two-door entrance with Esther Morris, antique dealer. Two doors down were Bradley ladies tailor and Hussey ladies hairdresser. Then two Miss Bobbetts, Peg and Clare, offered a costume and mantle service at no 13 while next door 'Annette' offered the more specialised 'picot edging'. This crochet trimming service was perhaps aimed not at the individual shopper but at the many top-quality dressmakers in the area, to achieve a more professional finish. The last few shops on that side of the Street were Arthur Senior, watchmaker, sharing no 16 with Hewson and Kay milliner and dressmaker. Peter Adamson made trunks, cases and bags in no 17 and sold them alongside Jenny Wren drapery. The last shop, on the corner with Dawson Street, was, like today, a man's clothier: then a merchant tailor. These were not all similarly sized businesses and their relative scale and location is indicated by the annual rents recorded in Thom's directory; Vine ladies tailor £12, Annette (picot edging) £21, Weir general textiles £125 and John Ryan boot and shoe maker £70. Cleo's rent is not recorded.[6]

On the opposite side of the Street were Deegan's newsagents whose premises, now a rare survivor, suggest the character and quality of the shop-fronts before most were later rebuilt or remodelled. Nearby a gown specialist

Cleo has always been located within the vicinity of Grafton Street, Dublin's most fashionable shopping Street, seen here c.1930 with the canopy of Switzers in the left foreground. Open and closed cars, trams, buses and bicycles share space on the cobbled street, while the paths are more crowded with pedestrians, each wearing a hat. (Courtesy Irish Architectural Archive.)

Deegan's shop front, South Anne Street. The double door, newspaper letterbox and asymmetrical windows suggest something of the character of Dublin's erstwhile shop fronts. Cleo's premises, on the other side of the street (of which no known image survives) were, according to Kitty, 'totally special. It was like a place you might find in a quiet street in Paris'.

worked upstairs, and following the Adelphi Billiard Rooms were two ladies' tailors – Vine and Herman Angel. Next, Mrs Howarth supplied cosmetics, perfume and remedies in no 24 and 'Isobel' - mantles and gowns - at no 25. On one corner of Anne's Lane was Nicholas Molloy's dairy and on the other was 'The Salon' a millinery, fur and gown salesroom (run by Katherine Hayes). Past Waddington Galleries (no 28) were Miss Ledwidge, milliner, 'Angeline' hairdresser and Nonie O'Meara purveying 'underclothing, jumpers etc', all sharing no 29. Then, no. 30 housed Beverly Smyth Removals and Storage as well as The Catholic Protection and Rescue Society and The St Vincent de Paul Society. Sharing no 31 were Miss McIntyre, professional corsetière, Miss Lily Bernstein, draper - and a furrier, Karel, operating just opposite Vard, which brought you back, past a fruiterer and florist on the corner, to Grafton Street.

KATHLEEN RYAN: DOMESTIC SKILLS AND CITY LIVING

Kathleen Ryan (née Crowe) had begun city life in the dress business in Switzers of Grafton Street, one of Dublin's earliest department stores, established in 1832. She was born in 1889 and grew up, one of ten children, on a farm in Gurtussa, Dundrum, South Tipperary. While all the Crowe girls were good knitters, she credited her particular needlework skills to the wonderful teacher in Annacarty National School who taught her crochet and lace as well as knitting and sewing. The National School curriculum offered all young girls a good basis in sewing and knitting, domestic skills equally valuable in any commercial dress department.

Kit Crowe, as her family knew her, apprenticed first in a shop in Tipperary town before coming to Dublin in 1912.

At the age of 23, Kit Crowe left Tipperary for Dublin to work in Switzers department store. The competition for any position in the drapery trade, even at apprentice level, is conveyed in an article, one of a series on job-seeking, run in *The Irish Press* at a time of scarce employment:

> Appointment as [draper's] apprentice however is not just a routine matter. Consideration of one's application involves an interview at which the employer must be satisfied as to the suitability of the applicant from the point of view of general appearance, bearing, speech, character. With a big number to choose from, it is understandable that a high standard in these matters is required... Promotion ... depends entirely on ability as against seniority in most other jobs.[7]

Though her daughter Kitty recalls no mention of any special prestige attaching to working in Switzers, other sources maintain that achieving such a position in one of the city's larger firms was a considerable coup and 'regarded as almost as secure as the Civil Service'. Even as an apprentice, which not only offered low wages but also often required a considerable 'security', to be paid (by the apprentice) to the business, such positions were

Kathleen (Kit) Crowe, was born (1889) not far from Cashel in South Tipperary. Photo c.1912.

A postcard sent to Kit Crowe at Miss Burke's, Tipperary, in 1911, picturing her friend boating near Boston. This young woman had also worked in Burke's but had emigrated to America. (Courtesy Mary Joyce)

84
A.BURKE
84

highly prized and usually dependent on an introduction.[8] No such introduction is recorded in Kit Crowe's case but it is worth considering that her home place, in South Tipperary, is close to the Limerick border, where the majority of Switzer families are also recorded in the 1911 census:

> Anyone acquainted with Dublin for the last twenty years must have seen with interest the gradual rise and development of the monster drapery house…[This] new extension now completed makes Switzer's an immense Emporium…
>
> The Costume and Millinery Department has been transformed into a splendid "salon", where ladies can view all the latest creations in gowns and chapeaux… An innovation in show rooms is the new artificially lighted department at one end of the Debutante's Costume Section, where ladies can see and judge for themselves the effect of artificial light on the different shades of color in the evening or ball dress. This should be greatly appreciated by fashionable women who know so well how a beautifully becoming color by daylight may be quite another shade, and very disappointing under artificial light, while a dainty, bespangled gown that may seem cold and tawdry in broad day light becomes a mass of shimmering splendour in the ballroom.[9]

Switzer's Debutantes' Costume Department, newly housed in 1912, the year Kit Crowe came to work there, in a large and glamorous extension. This expansion resulted in Switzers occupying a site stretching from Grafton Street, to Wicklow Street to Clarendon Street. (Courtesy Irish Architectural Archive, and with thanks for the reference to Dr. Ellen Rowley, Trinity College Dublin).

Opposite: Burke's Millinery, 84 Henry Street, Tipperary Town c. 1909, where Kathleen Crowe, (second left), first worked in the clothing trade. As a milliner in her early 20s, she not only worked for, but also lodged with Miss Annie Burke, Miss Burke's younger sister, and a domestic servant, Bridget O'Brien, at 31 William O'Brien Street, Tipperary Town. (Photo courtesy Mary Joyce).

From Switzers Kit Crowe moved to work in Ranelagh, to a dressmaking and drapery business, Cathcart, owned by two sisters.

Her experience developed there when she was put in charge of many aspects of the business from orders, to sales and accounts. Asked to take sole charge of operations while the sisters were away for some time, Kit Crowe attended to every detail, but, 'when the sisters returned and quibbled about a single penny, she gave in her notice with rage'.

Instead of seeking another position her entrepreneurial instincts steered her towards enterprises of her own. She began in Molesworth Street employing 'two very good milliners' and through the 1920s supplied clothes and hats to customers many of whom had followed her from Switzers and from Cathcart's. Already from this time her clientele had an international reach; hat boxes posted to tropical destinations were packed with special black tissue to protect the headwear from humidity and mildew as they were shipped across the equator.

A NEW STATE: MARRIAGE & BUSINESS

In the late 1920s Kit Crowe married Bryan Ryan who, like her, was from a farming background in Tipperary. He ran two spirit grocer businesses in Dublin. One,

Cathcart's millinery in Ranelagh in the early 20th Century, with Kit Crowe standing at left in the doorway. (Photo courtesy Mary Joyce).

close to Broadstone Station, was 'rather like a mini Smyth's on the Green' (the renowned food emporium on St. Stephen's Green) the other was more ordinary. But in the early 1930s his business, like so many others, declined badly with the international Depression and then Ireland's trade war with Britain; the mid 1930s saw Ireland's cattle trade destroyed when Britain, Ireland's main customer, boycotted imports as a response to De Valera withholding land annuities. These economic circumstances forced the Ryan family to move to the smaller business at 21 Abercorn Road in East Wall. Pressure on them increased when, following a practice Kitty says was not unusual among hard pressed farming families, two female relations were sent to stay with Bryan in Dublin 'to help' with his business. Although only recently married, and with their only child, Kitty, his wife responded to their situation by borrowing £25 from her brother-in-law to set up again, as a dressmaker, opening in rooms above a smart tobacconist opposite Trinity College.

The Depression and Economic War persisted and, in 1936, Mrs Ryan was approached by an estate agent with the suggestion her dressmaking might do better in ground floor premises rather than upstairs, and was offered, at a reasonable rent, two rooms with a shop window at 10 South Anne Street. The premises had recently been vacated by a South African woman who had traded for only six weeks, but before opening had a sign-writer paint the name 'Cleo' above the door. Mrs Ryan saw little point in the expense of having the 'Cleo' removed and after several years it would seem her business came to be known by that name; In *Thom's Directory* for 1941 she is listed as 'Kathleen Ryan dressmaker' but some years later she appears as 'Cleo Gowns'. 'Dressmakers' could be found all over the city, often working from home, but a purveyor of 'gowns' was more metropolitan.

An advertisment for Slyne & Co., situated opposite the junction where South Anne Street meets Grafton Street, just a stone's throw from Cleo. The work of Kit Ryan (Crowe) would now be seen in the context of the best Dublin had to offer.

Close to Cleo, at 71 Grafton Street, the great purveyor of 'gowns' was Eileen Slyne, a dressmaker and another shrewd businesswoman:

> In the 1920s and Thirties she would go to the fashion shows in Paris. They searched people attending in order to take away their pencils and paper. She would hide her pencil in the ladies and during breaks dash out and scribble down the designs. A week later she would have clothes based on these designs in the window of Slyne's.[10]

Although only a minority might afford her prices, Slyne's window at least offered regular and up-to-date news from Paris. Window-shopping, particularly at night time, had long been a pleasurable pastime in Dublin. Shop windows were lit up and dressed with goods, often labelled and priced. That is until the 1970s and 80s when the advent of metal shutters turned urban streets grey after dark.

Mrs Ryan's 'Cleo' dressmaking and gown business consisted of herself, in the front room dealing with customers, and a 'wonderful, loyal but rather over chatty Mrs Lyons, from Bandon, in the back room on a sewing machine.' Since striking out on her own Kit Ryan had maintained the sort of clientele she knew from her time in Switzers. 'Sporting hats in the windows, well-cut tweed suits and hand-worked linen blouses', Switzers was regarded as 'the very home of Anglo-Irish clothes.[11] And that is in a city where every business, club or organisation had a distinct profile as either Catholic or Protestant (a feature of Irish life persisting until the 1960s).'[12] Mrs Ryan herself characterised her customers in Switzers as 'Colonels' ladies' and in South Anne Street she retained the loyalty of this mainly Anglo-Irish clientele; a group long characterised by a taste for tweeds and wools, serviceable against wind and rain, and long established as functional outdoor wear. The same robust fabrics have proven equally invaluable against indoor breezes and chill in the draughty spaces inhabited by many of the gentry long after most suburban houses enjoyed the comforts of central heating.

In the early years of Irish political independence from Britain, producers of Irish wool struggled to compete with foreign imports leading the Free-State government (1922–1949) to support local production through the restriction of cheaper imports and promotion of Irish goods. For most hard-pressed buyers however price was the determining factor, therefore manufacturers and retailers pushed for more imported cloth to supply this trade:

> A number of [manufacturing] firms who have exhausted the import quota for the first period claim that they cannot economically use Irish material for cheap suitings and that fresh supplies of imported cloth cannot be obtained until after July 31. The minister is being asked to allow the importation of further supplies...
>
> [According to a Dublin man's shop on South Great George's Street] the firm had endeavoured to meet the situation by instructing their salesmen to sell at least three suits of Irish material in every four sold, but the public had not responded.[13]

These economic circumstances and consumer choices meant the continued decline in Irish spinning and weaving:

> At the end of the First World War there were 80 mills in operation in what was to be the new state. Ten years later, after the Depression, only half of these remained, mostly the small mills... The decline in fortune of the mills was to continue, erratically but inevitably.
>
> The period between the wars, however, saw a renewal of the revival of thirty years earlier in the handwoven area. In 1927, the three Wynne sisters of Avoca in County Wicklow started a small handspun, hand dyed, handwoven operation... The Farrells, Michael and Frances, also produced featherweight materials in rich colours at their Crock of Gold Studio [in Blackrock, Co.Dublin],
>
> In 1936 the Irish Homespun Society was formed, Dr. Muriel Gahan being one of the guiding forces.[14]

As part of the redress of this decline, in 1951 the Minister for Education, Richard Mulcahy, established a weaving course at The National College of Art, with the aim of building on the craft revival and attempting to support an industry deeply embedded in the life and economy of the country. To run the department he

FROM LADY BIRLEY. CHARLESTON MANOR. WESTDEAN, SEAFORD, SUSSEX. Tel. ALFRISTON 267 (0321 82 267)

Dear Mrs. Ryan, 16 December, 1971

Thank you for your letter, and also two very nice green skirts which have arrived safely. Would you please send me 1½ yards of the green material, and also save another 1½ yards which Lady Drogheda may want? I will ask her at Christmas about this, and write to you early in the New Year.

With all good wishes,

Yours sincerely,

Rhoda Birley

Lady Rhoda Birley was a customer highly regarded by Cleo. A noted Irish beauty, she married in England. The quality of Kit Ryan's product and service ensured the loyalty of her clientele, even after they had long moved abroad.

Rhoda Birley was described by Lady Diana Cooper as 'heavenly – full of goodness and absolutely guileless'. Lady Birley was also mother of celebrated beauty Maxime, and grandmother of Lou Lou de la Falaise, the model, designer and muse of Yves Saint Laurent.[15] (Photograph, by Valerie Finnis, courtesy of The Royal Horticultural Society.)

appointed Lillias Mitchell, herself part of that interwar revival of crafts. In the 1940s she had opened a studio-weaving workshop, The Golden Fleece, in 84 Lower Mount Street, Dublin.

WIDOWHOOD, WAR & WOOL

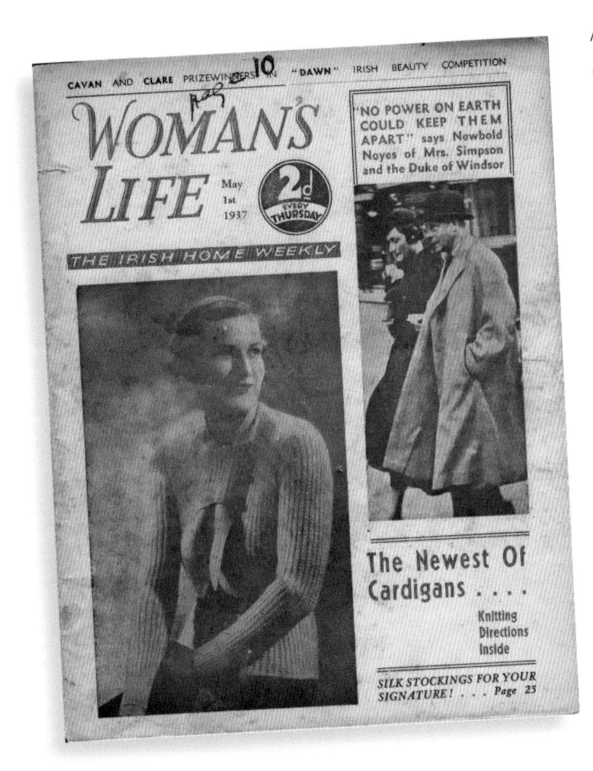

Woman's Life, 1 May 1937. Magazines, both the more and less expensive, included knitting patterns promising fashionable new looks. And despite nationalist sentiment, Ireland's popular magazines, as much then as now, suggest a great public interest in the lives of the British Royal family.

Although neutral during World War II, Ireland was of course still greatly affected by restrictions brought on by the conflict. Into the 1930s British ships had transported most goods to Ireland, but with these (and British manufacture) now committed to the war effort there was a greatly reduced capacity for production or transport of food, fabrics or fashions throughout Britain let alone to Ireland. In response, as in Britain, a coupon and rationing system was implemented to control and husband resources. Shop owners, as much as customers, were restricted to their coupon allocation and even for the wealthy access to key commodities was, at least theoretically, limited by the equitable coupon system.

Restrictions and wartime shortages did not deter Mrs Ryan who supplemented what stock she could buy with her own hand-crocheted pieces to liven up the window in South Anne Street. Crochet was Kit Ryan's particular skill though it was hand knitting which, by the 1930s, provided many women with a relatively economic and accessible source of fashionable separates.

Women knitted at home using shop bought wool and invented or inherited patterns, or they worked from the popular pattern-instructions published in weekly magazines. Even among schoolgirls, the boarders in Roscrea, for example, it is remembered that 'During the 1930s, the "in thing" was knitting – at recreation, the senior girls took the craze very seriously.'[16] A new prestige attached to knitwear since the Prince of Wales had taken to wearing a Fair Isle sweater to play the fashionable game of golf. Throughout Free State Ireland many women took pride in producing this 'royal' garment for their men folk.

But as the war ground on even shop-bought wool became difficult to source. Homespun wool however was not included under government restriction or rationing and here Mrs Ryan saw a possible solution to her dwindling stock. She could not personally travel the country to source farmer's wool, having the shop to run and her daughter to rear alone, as she had recently been widowed.

As her circumstances declined along with supplies Mrs Ryan had started taking lodgers to supplement her income. Rather than lean on the newly formed government for a widow's pension she determined to survive on her own efforts and rented large premises behind Findlater's shop at 302 Lower Rathmines Road. Among her lodgers was a man known as 'Irishman Tuohy' (to distinguish him from 'The Chemist Tuohy'). Irishman Tuohy loved the West of Ireland and could

Three generations of a family in Northwest Ireland (1950s). The father of the young child wears a Fair Isle sleeveless sweater knit for him by his wife (back row right). Pleased with the result she complimented him that he 'looked like a Royal' wearing it. [17] (Courtesy Clare Drury, whose grandmother, Margaret Cullen, is the skilled knitter).

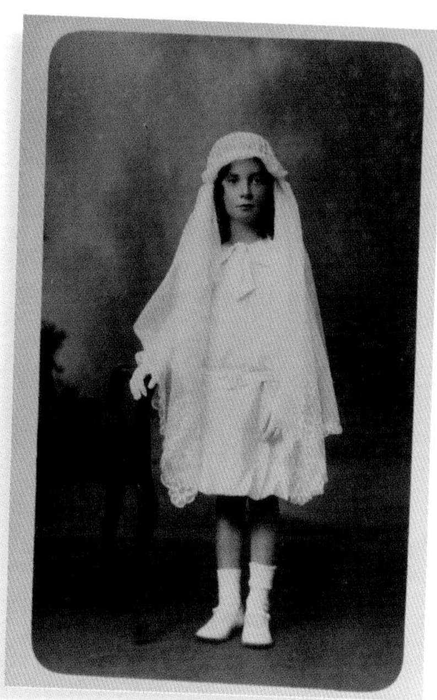

At a time of general economic hardship (c.1937) Kit Ryan's daughter, Kitty, is photographed on her First Holy Communion day in a hand-made dress and crocheted headdress. Until relatively recently women's sewing, knitting and crochet skills helped turn out beautifully presented children on such special occasions.

not bear the city in the summer, so each year in the good weather he headed off to work the land. Mrs Ryan asked him to keep an eye out for knitters who might contact her. As a result several women did send samples of their work and when she liked them she asked for one or two more similar pieces. What had begun as an immediate solution to a pressing dilemma was to become a relationship that would change the nature of her business.

From now on, as much as being a maker herself, Kit Ryan would develop as a creative commissioner directing and collaborating with other craft workers.

To select the work she wanted a practice of requesting samples became her norm. But it is a tricky business at a distance. It soon became clear that women skilled in knitting gloves, for example, might not produce socks to the same standard. Over time the system, particularly for finding women to knit Aran sweaters, was refined to requesting samples of sweaters - with sleeves - because it emerged that women who could knit a sweater with well-set sleeves tended to be the most skilful knitters. If a garment was good Mrs Ryan would ask for another.

While schoolgirls throughout Ireland learned basic knitting, skills beyond mechanical competence were more rare. What Mrs Ryan sought was creativity and knitting that was lyrical rather than simply utilitarian. And, having selected the best knitters, Cleo was regularly rewarded with magical pieces. One particular example, that went on to become a best seller in Cleo, was the *crios* hat, which arrived one day amidst a delivery from The Aran Islands, posted in a flour bag.

The *crios* hat, a highly inventive creation of the late 1940s or early '50s from Maggie Dirrane, on the Aran Islands. The work combines a woven *crios*, a knitted crown and crochet edging all put together in harmonious colours. (Courtesy Cleo)

The hat was created by a knitter Kitty describes as 'one of the island's most creative knitters, Maggie Dirrane, mother of the poet Máirtín Ó Direáin', and a woman regarded by her daughter as, more or less, the 'inventor' of the Aran stitch.

Such imaginative engagement with local materials and skills had almost come to be expected from the Aran Islands since John Millington Synge, Jack Yeats and John (later Seán) Keating captured the depth of tradition surviving into the early 20th century in Island life on the west coast of Ireland. [18] But this sort of creative freedom and invention with wool was threatened almost as soon as it was recognised. With knitwear becoming fashionable in the 1930s and '40s, a government enterprise, Gaeltarra Éireann, sought to capitalise on its popularity and on knitting skills around the country. To speed up and regularise production they issued factory-spun wool and uniform patterns throughout Ireland to skilled women who, once they got used to the stitches of 'cable down the centre, with diamonds on either side', were expected to produce a sweater a week to maintain their place as a Gaeltarra knitter. Already by 1945 Muriel Gahan, the great promoter and spokeswoman for Irish crafts, was worried about this destruction of individual creativity among knitters.[19]

In direct contrast to this standardised work Cleo particularly encouraged the unusual and individual. Often the samples received were designs women had 'knit from their head' and occasionally might have highly skilful knitting but 'crazy shapes'. In these cases Cleo would return the sample with written or sketched instructions for improving the piece. When Maggie Dirrane's daughter, Dympna, began to act as Cleo's agent on Aran mór, she made the initial selection, and sweaters then came in 'wonderful shapes'. This patient and responsive attention repaid Mrs Ryan with contributors able to supply more original and superior knits to her shop.

There was a gulf between the situations inhabited by Cleo and its first knitters. The different worlds were suggested in the letters Kitty recalls accompanying the knitting, asking to be paid not in cash, but in something like a pair of Wellington boots. It may be that the knitters pictured any shop selling woollens as the kind familiar throughout the country selling shovels and nails as well as tea, milk, overalls, jumpers and drapery.

In Cleo, despite being better stocked and a little livelier during the War than neighbouring shops, custom was still very slow, to the extent that it often seemed hardly worth opening. Kitty recalls helping her mother by minding the shop and over a few days the only customer she had was a gentleman ordering a pair of socks – which Kitty knit for him herself. So, rather than wait for custom to come to them Cleo went out to find it and achieved a small increase in sales through advertising in an English magazine of the countryside, *The Field*. By the time the

War was over Cleo had become comfortable with native home-produced wools and so had their customers and knitwear and homespun became the stock-in-trade for which they have since developed an international reputation.

But then, just as business began to rebuild after the war and interest in her clothes was emerging among new American tourists, her landlord's widow put No. 10 South Anne Street up for sale. By 1950, therefore, Mrs Ryan's custom and business were in transition on several fronts; she was moving shop and her mainstay was no longer dressmaking (often for 'awkward figures') among a small Anglo-Irish clientele, but supplying hand knitting to a wider range of buyers. In her early years of business what Kit Ryan had offered her customer was something like a small version of Switzers dress department; by the end of the War her shop could be seen as closer to the sort of 'Irish Industry' enterprises encouraged by the Fianna Fáil protectionist policies. She was moving from serving a more local elite with bespoke clothing to offering a rural vernacular dress to international visitors.

Though she had come to this Irish product along her own particular path, shaped by her home, school, personal circumstances and war time exigencies this market was already inhabited by bigger and more strategically established players. Advertising in the *Saorstat Éireann Handbook* (1932) gives some sense of the sort of commercial and cultural context in which Cleo grew up. 'Everything Irish' was how the Gaeltacht Industries Ltd advertised themselves at 39 Nassau

Advertising in Ireland's Free-State Handbook, *Saorstat Éireann* (1932) numerous businesses promoted themselves highlighting the Irishness of their product.

Street (close to where the tour buses now stop and park) and where Kennedy & McSharry have long sold characteristically 'country clothing'. The Leinster Hand Weaving Company Ltd had substantial premises at 103 Grafton Street, close to the junction with Suffolk Street. The Country Shop was at 23 Saint Stephen's Green and The Hand Loom Shop at no 133. Irish Cottage Industries Ltd 'securing the cream of Tweeds' was at 6 Dawson Street and Kevin & Howlin first opened just a door or two away from their current premises. While Kevin & Howlin (also est. 1936 and known mainly for men's clothes) remains almost the grandfather of that stretch of tourist shops along Nassau Street, it, unlike Cleo (known mainly for women's wear) has enjoyed the custom of local Irish people as well as tourists. Perhaps the image of the Irish countryman has had wider appeal throughout the 20th century than its counterpart: the Irish countrywoman.

Endnotes

1 (1984) Virago Press, pp. 149-150.

2 Costello, P. and T. Farmar (1992) *The Very Heart of the City, The Story of Denis Guiney and Clery's, Dubin*, A & A Farmar.

Costello, P. (2008) *Denis Guiney*, Dublin, UCD Press.

Haverty, A (1995) *Elegant Times, A Dublin Story*, Dublin, Sonas.

Nesbitt, Ronald (1993) *At Arnotts of Dublin*, Dublin, A & A Farmar.

Rains, Stephanie (2010) *Commodity, Culture & Social Class in Dublin 1850-1916*, Dublin, Irish Academic Press.

3 Daly, Mary E. (1992) *Industrial Development and Irish National Identity, 1922-1939*, Dublin, Gill and Macmillan, pp. 42-43.

4 See Burman, Barbara (1999) *The Culture of Sewing: Gender, Consumption and Home Dressmaking*, Oxford, Berg. Also Sheridan, John (May, 1958) 'Bespoke Clothing', *Creation*, unpaginated.

5 O'Kelly, Hilary, in conversation with Bob Sower, Department of Textiles, NCAD 2011.

6 *Thom's Directory* (1941) pp 868-869.

7 *Irish Press* (23/11/1949) 'Any Jobs going? How To Be Draper's Assistant' p. 2.

8 Farmar, Tony (1995) *Ordinary Lives; The private lives of three generations of Ireland's professional classes*, A&A Farmar, Dublin, p.89.

9 *Irish Life* (6 December 1912) 'Switzer's New Showrooms' pp.337 - 340.

10 Ryan, Vera (2010), *Movers and Shapers 3*, in conversation with Ian Whyte, Galley Head Press, Cork, p. 133.

11 Farmar, Tony (1995) *op. cit.*, p. 102.

12 Ibid. pp. 81-82.

13 *The Irish Press* (6. June 1935) p. 3.

14 Sutton, Frank (1980) *Weaving The Irish Inheritance*, Gilbert Dalton, Dublin, p.45.

15 Lau, Venessa (25 October 2010) *WWD*, www.wwd.com/fashion-news/fashion-features/july-22-1976-portrait.

16 *Convent of The Sacred Heart, Roscrea. 1842–1992.* Prior/Cunningham p. 95.

17 Drury, Clare (2006) *Handknit in rural Ireland (1940–1960)*, unpublished thesis NCAD.

18 See Kennedy, B.P. & R. Gillespie (1994) *Ireland, Art into History*. Also Scott, Yvonne, (2005) *The West as Metaphor*, RHA, Dublin.

19 Mitchell, Geraldine (1997) *Deeds Not Words*, Town House, Dublin, p. 89.

MOLESWORTH STREET

Becoming Cleo – Handknits and Handweaves

With the sale of the shop in South Anne Street c. 1950, Mrs Ryan had to look for new premises. Naturally she wanted to remain in the area she had known almost 40 years since her Switzers days in 1912, and she found a suitable place in the basement of a Georgian building at No. 3 Molesworth Street. Now aged 61, she decided on a 21-year lease, as she did not expect the business to continue beyond her own time; her daughter Kitty, determined 'to do something useful' with her working life, had chosen nursing and was accepted into the Mater Hospital in 1949.

But as her mother became older and busier Kitty increasingly helped out in the shop, with the result that her 'nursing résumé was becoming patchy'. In 1955, by then aware that 'all work is useful', she decided to make the break with nursing and commit full time to Cleo where she says 'a love affair began and still endures'.

Aran Sweaters
for Men, Women
and Children
Tams. Socks,
Gloves, Hand
Woven Rugs,
Scarves and
Kinsale Cloaks

Phone CLEO 73408
Mrs. Ryan, Proprietress
3 MOLESWORTH ST.,
DUBLIN.
Opposite Hibernian Hotel
Wholesale & Retail

A Cleo business card from the 1960s.

LOCATION & STOCK

Molesworth Street, originally part of a planned centrepiece to Dublin's 18th century urban landscape, has changed considerably, in character and in use, even since the 1950s. Then, on one side, it remained lined with Georgian buildings and

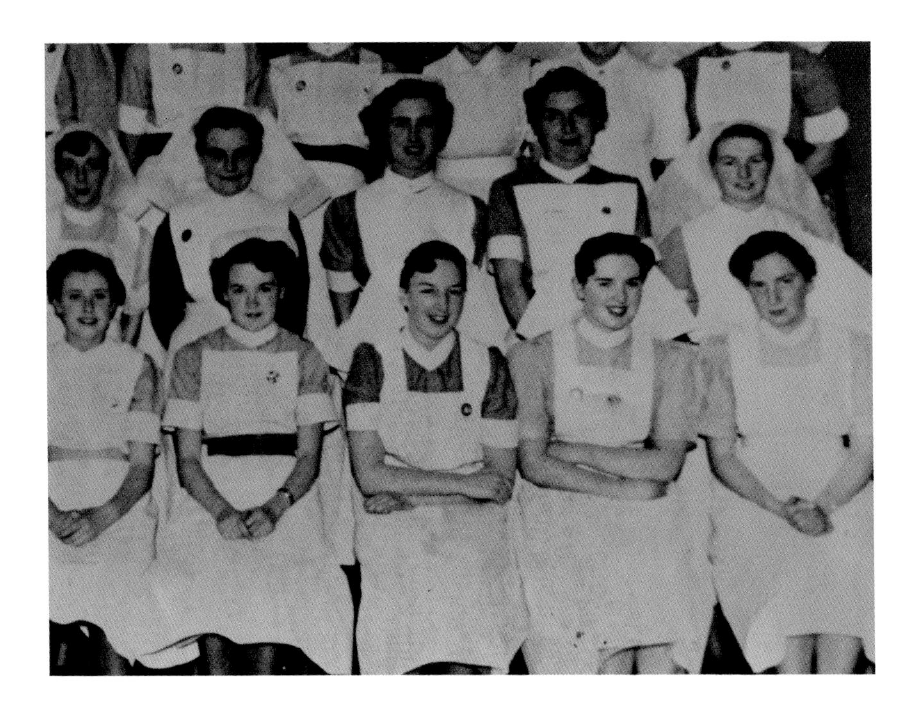

Kitty Joyce (née Ryan), bottom right, on the staff of the Mater Hospital c. 1950.

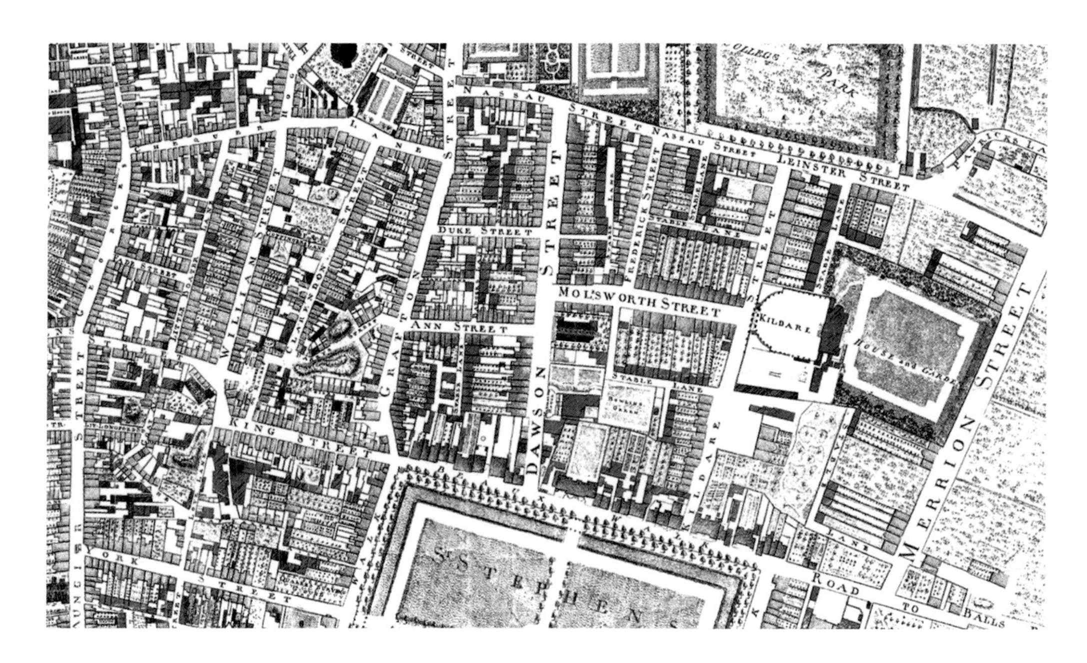

Cleo has always been situated in what has been described as 'the most prestigious network of streets in Dublin city. Their blend of state, institutional, commercial and residential uses imbues the area with a distinctive identity and civic sense that is instantly recognisable as a major component of the heart of the capital'[1]

on the other stood the highly ornamental, neo-Gothic St Anne's School and Hall, by Deane and Woodward. The steps down to the Georgian basement occupied by Cleo were just where the post box still stands close to the junction of Dawson Street from where 'the magnificent vista of Leinster House is best experienced.'[2] While today that part of the street comprises of mainly bland 1970s office buildings, in the 1950s the Georgian town houses were a continuation of the shopping district of Grafton and Dawson Street along with a mix of restaurants as well as legal and accountancy firms.

Directly opposite Cleo, for example, Kitty remembers 'a joy' of a fabric shop piled high with bolts of neatly rolled and regularly sized fabrics in resplendent colours and a range of weights and textures. 'There would be two lines of customers up against the counter – and maybe a third behind them'. Next door to Cleo was a shop selling knitting yarn, well selected, by a woman – herself a great knitter – who traded as Miss R. Kennedy, art needlework and fancy wool warehouse. [3] In the basement opposite Cleo was a 'very gifted' headdress maker, Carmel Skeehan, a graduate of The National College of Art, trading under the sign of 'The Orchid Wedding Headdress, Model Flowers'. She was one of many who continued to earn a living as a milliner in an age when a 'respectable' person was still considered 'undressed' without a hat. Mary Colwin, ladies dress designer and tailor occupied No. 4, along with a solicitor, while Bentley's Restaurant shared No. 5 with an antique dealer. The Dreadnought School of Fashion was housed in part of No. 6 Molesworth Street and around the corner on South Frederick Street the Grafton Academy of Fashion Design had been opened by Pauline Clotworthy, in 1938.

During her early years in business Mrs Ryan had made her own crocheted pieces to supplement the dress stock in South Anne Street, limited by wartime shortages. Now, as the knitwear side burgeoned, the process reversed and Cleo began to source clothing to complement the knitwear in Molesworth Street. A new vision, therefore, was taking shape in Cleo, where a focus on local rural produce grew out of Mrs Ryan's country background and skills turned to advantage during wartime necessity.

After the war this work met a wave of appreciation from visitors to Ireland – from the United States and Britain. To emphasise the emerging image of their enterprise, when Kitty joined the business, she travelled up and down to Galway, to Ó Máille, sourcing for instance the collarless báinín jackets of the Aran Islands. She also sought out shawls worn in the Aran Islands. By the 1950s they were scarce and difficult to find, but through advertising in the Galway papers some could be found second-hand. This was a supply system that survived until 1961, but then there were no more replies to their advertisements.

KNITTERS & KNITTING

As demand grew for her stock after the war, more knitters were needed, and to find them, Mrs Ryan set off for Donegal with a cousin who owned a Volkswagen Beetle. Donegal may have been chosen because the county was especially known since the 1880s for hand knitting, and before that for weaving. When she arrived in any village over the years, Mrs Ryan 'would go to the water pump, where women were known to gather, to inquire about knitters'. Her success on one venture is evident in the Cleo order books of 1955 and 1956 which are filled with names and addresses of women in the village of Ballintra, many of whom have garments attached to their names indicating the woman's particular skill or inclination: 'May Sweeney for socks' or 'Grace Friel for ladies sweaters'.

The knitting skills in the Donegal village of Ballintra must have been due, in part, to the philanthropy of a Mrs Hamilton, who in the 1880s and '90s (like many Anglo-Irish women) assisted households in the area develop a source of income through a cottage industry in domestic needlework. Knitting may be regarded as having been almost a universal Irish woman's skill, but not everybody had the inclination, patience or skills to knit, or at least to knit well. Others loved knitting and were unhappy when they had 'nothing on the needles'. The ambiguous status of knitting between labour and pleasure prompted one little boy recently to ask his Donegal grandmother if knitting was like work or play? She had to think about it before replying that, to her, it was like play but that when finished you have achieved something and have some work done.[4]

Girls and young women who were so inclined could, by the 1930s and '40s, learn knitting at National School, at home or from the teachers employed around the country by the government to train women to knit for Gaeltarra Eireann.[5] These government schools, run by the Department of Agriculture and Technical Instruction (established 1899),[6] grew out of the work of the Congested Districts Board and philanthropic enterprises, like those of Mrs Hamilton. Convents were

Patchwork blanket created as a gift from 'squares' contributed by amateur knitters of all ages from Ireland and abroad, c. 2002. (Private collection).

also places where knitting was taught and produced, often to a high standard. Although this was a widely known and valued source of handwork in Ireland it is a practice that now appears a great deal less benign than it did even ten years ago, and remains an aspect of Irish society, design and material culture yet to be researched. The aim of many government supported schemes for knitting remained that of offering women a means of supplementing the family income and that is what many women did, as well as knitting clothes that would keep their own families warm, respectable and even stylish.

Here it might be argued that a scale of knitting skills emerged ranging from the 'master' knitter to the amateur. Those with more experience and learning who took pleasure in knitting could master an understanding of materials and techniques. They could read a piece of knitting or imagine a garment and produce it. The amateur on the other hand knows the stitches and can follow a pattern, some with little feeling for the materials or technique, others with great technical skill. Amateur work declares its domestic origins loudly but the more advanced a skill becomes, the more any trace of the making disappears. As Glenn Adamson points out skill 'is most conspicuous in its absence'.[7]

The significance of knitting as a source of income in County Donegal is reflected in Brian Friel's *Dancing at Lughnasa* (1990) where the livelihood of Maggie's four sisters is made through knitting. Their fragile living however collapses in 1936, when a machine-knitting factory opens in the local Donegal town. Indeed the arrival of the knitting machine threatened local production in many communities and one response of hand-knitters and promoters, not only in Ireland, was to emphasise the 'ethnic' and 'original' qualities of their produce. In 1956 Muriel Gahan, introduced a 'Hand Made in Aran' label to identify the work she sold in The Country Shop as specifically of island origin. The result of this marketing strategy was, out of necessity, developing a very local and minor practice into a substantial regional industry.[8]

In his writing about Aran, J.M. Synge observed how the spirit of the West of Ireland was embodied in the objects that surrounded its people.[10] Hand knitting and weaving came to be seen as integral to the Aran identity. It is little surprise then that these fabrics, with the smell of lanolin and turf fires in the fibres, became signifiers of the romance of the West of Ireland, and, in turn, desirable as souvenirs of a visit to a special place. A hand-knitted Aran sweater, knit anywhere in Ireland, could be seen as a material embodiment of the separation between pre-industrial society of the West of Ireland and modern, urban consumerism. Wool is particularly evocative in this role, sheep and shepherds having:

> played the starring role in ancient pastoral literature, not only because they stayed in the fields all day but because their profession predated the dawn of

Opposite: Cleo handknit and crios hat, photographed by Mike Bunn in Delphi Valley, Co. Mayo. Models; Tijam, and Millie Mantle, daughter of proprietor of Delphi lodge, where the group stayed during the shoot c. 1993.

Guus Melai for Fógra Fáilte and Aer Lingus: *Ireland Invites You*, 1953.

Representation of an Aran fisherman, dressed in locally made clothes of the sort sold by Cleo. He is shown both weaving and wearing a crios belt, along with homespun trousers (known in Cleo as fisherman's trousers), pampooties, an Aran handknit sweater and a tam-o-shanter cap.

Ireland's tourist board and Aer Lingus (est. 1936) joined in promoting the country as a pastoral idyll surviving in the jet age. The resulting imagery – a carefully wrought 'cultural instrument'[9] – was perhaps aimed at assuaging anxieties in an increasingly mechanised society.

(Courtesy The National Museum of Ireland).

> civilization and law. The shepherd is, then, an allegorical figure, who stands for removal not only from the city but also from history itself. The countryside that the shepherd inhabits is an asylum that even in earliest pastoral poems, seems to be in the process of slipping away.[12]

For a visitor immersed in a country and valuing the depth of this relationship, the cheap mass-produced souvenir represents a lamentable offering. 'This purist purchases not only a garment, but the tradition and history and the trace of the maker, place and time that goes into every stitch.'[13] Knowing their Irish garment is the work of an individual hand and household - and not the anonymous product of an urban factory – is what some seek and are happy to pay for. Through finding individual hand-knitters all over the country Cleo has built up a reputation for this quality over decades.

For Cleo identifying skilled knitters was the first step in the involved process of sourcing handmade goods from rural Ireland to sell in Dublin. Once identified, each knitter was sent, by post to her home, the wool required for her garment – and in return the knitter posted a sweater about three weeks later. If living in Dublin the knitter might collect the yarn from the shop and return the work in person. This meeting between maker and commissioner afforded an opportunity to discuss the piece and make suggestions for the next one. According to one knitter, Betty Hewitt, with experience of knitting for different firms, in Cleo her work and experience were exceptionally appreciated and respected and she was paid immediately.[14]

These arrangements sound a little more sympathetic than those practiced by larger-scale operations, according to Donegal knitter Mary McNelis:

> Gaeltarra used to come with a lorry load of yarn, every week. And all the weavers and knitters would go to collect their bags of yarn for weaving or knitting jumpers in their own homes.
>
> 'You had to stand for two hours in a queue to get yarn. It was always on a Thursday you went. And the garment you left on the previous Thursday was the one you'd get paid for. In the meantime, the jumpers were sent to Galway where they were checked for flaws. If there was the slightest fault, instead of your money coming back, your garment came back. You had to correct whatever was wrong before you were paid.'[15]

Aran knitting is recognised around the world and, even in Ireland, often regarded as something of a national dress.[16] Belief in its historic authenticity was widespread in the 1950s and, as Cleo grew more and more closely identified with Aran knitwear, Kit Ryan and Kitty were intrigued to know what the knitters from Aran themselves had to say about its origins. They asked Dympna Dirrane, an expert knitter, and the agent for Cleo on Aran mór. She wrote back relating how her mother, Maggie Dirrane (the creator of the crios hat) had emigrated to America in the early 20th century and there developed her knitting skills, learning complex stitches under the influence of women from different parts of the world. On her return to Aran she adapted these stitches to incorporate the forms she saw around her, including baskets, honeycombs, ropes and blackberries. It was such creativity, shared by other women on the islands, that gave rise to the báinín knits of the 1930s and 1940s and so rapidly became the physical expression of a mythical past. The letter containing Dympna's account was treasured in Cleo, and framed for safekeeping. But it was kept facing the wall in the shop, aware as the Cleo women were what a great deal of the Irish economy 'was hanging on that story'.

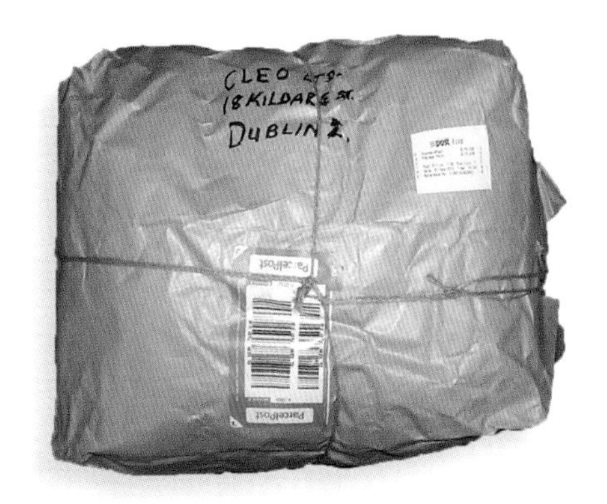

Painstakingly wrapped parcels of handmade goods arrive in Cleo. Photographed by Maureen Lewis, assistant and charming prescence in Cleo for sixteen years (1996–2012).

CAROL BROWN AND EARLY EXPORT, THE 1950S

It is now widely understood that finding export markets for local goods is essential for Ireland's economic health. Cleo's early years in business however coincided with the Fianna Fáil government's ideals of self-sufficiency, prioritising import substitution and protectionism over the creation of bigger markets. Internal trade rather than export was the focus of policy. And indeed between 1936 and the mid 1950s Cleo's business centred on retail custom and bespoke orders, transacted in the shop. But as Mrs Ryan recognised, survival would depend on building markets abroad, and she in fact had been posting Irish goods to the Tropics in the 1920s and 30s and to Britain and America since the 1940s.

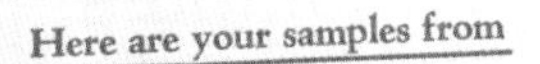

Here are your samples from

CAROL BROWN, PUTNEY, VERMONT 05346

I hope they interest you. They were painstakingly chosen; there are many more.

Please return them with your comments and suggestions if you want others. Please return them anyway, as they are precious and must continue to travel for me. PLEASE.

Carol Brown, mentor, friend and first export partner of Cleo in America, ran her Vermont business with an equally personalised, independent and original style.

What was to turn their one-off piecemeal business into a more robust export trade was Cleo's encounter with Carol Brown, who would become a most important and enduring American customer and their first wholesale partner. Carol Brown first visited Ireland in 1926 on a cycling trip and became deeply enamoured of the country and its woollen cloths. Throughout her very long life, in Boston and Vermont, she became a highly influential ambassador for Ireland and especially for Irish wools.

Concentrating on outstanding imported fabrics from Ireland and India she ran a renowned oasis of quality materials from her home in Putney, Vermont, where architects, designers and politicians came, not only for her fabrics, but also for her views and advice. Something of her influence and commitment to Ireland can be seen in what Kitty claims was her steering the World Crafts Council to hold one of its first gatherings in Dublin, in 1970. Like Cleo, her business was a natural extension of her love of handmade cloths and those who made and valued them.

In the Cleo archive one or two undated newspaper cuttings record appreciation for Carol Brown's atmospheric and distinctive business:

Everything about Carol Brown's work had the mark of the handmade and individual - from her promotional material to the shop itself - which she ran from her home with her nephew Laurie.

We don't worship the Almighty Dollar here,' says a chipper, 88 year old Carol. 'We have a very intimate personal place'...

Those all too used to turning turnstiles at J.C. Penney's or bustling through crowds at Bloomingdale's find Carol and Lawrie's shop an oasis in the madness of shopperdom

...It's not odd to find both beat up Volkswagens and highly polished Mercedes parked in the driveway, with licence plates from as far away as Alaska, California or Florida.

Avid "fabric freaks" may have heard of the place through friends or else in catalogues geared to materials –"Old House Catalogue" and "First Home Decorators" for instance.[17]

For all its alternative informality, Carol Brown's was, like Cleo's, a highly regarded and well-connected enterprise. Having much in common they nurtured business and creative relations on the subjects of tweed, wool and hand knits. Carol and Kitty travelled extensively through Ireland to find makers and materials, but also abroad – to Peru for instance, and with the interest created in Nordic countries by 'The Scandinavian Report', to Finland. They swapped information on natural fabrics, organic foods, shiatsu massage and macrobiotic diets. Kitty says 'Carol Brown was my university'. None of this – the independence, travel or interests – reflects anything of the stereotype of the inward Ireland of Archbishop McQuaid or De Valera in the 1950s.

IRISH CLOTHES & INTERNATIONAL DESIGN

An atmosphere closer to that stereotype does seem to have been achieved by the Irish government when promoting goods at home. As part of their strategy to showcase Irish production in a protected environment, the Government had opened a Permanent Exhibition of Irish Manufacturers, at 3 St. Stephen's Green, close to the top of Grafton Street. Kitty remembers it around the 1950s as 'a long dark space, lined with glass cases that felt like something from The Soviet Union'. It was presided over by 'a rather severe-looking woman', Mrs O'Connor (a widow, whose daughter Mairin later married hurler and Taoiseach, Jack Lynch).[18] This display of Irish goods was an initiative on the part of NAIDA, the National Agricultural and Industrial Association (est. 1929) a body that emerged in the wake of the Federation of Saorstat Industries.[19] With a wide brief, NAIDA oversaw not only the promotion of agriculture, but also the Dublin Saint Patrick's day parade, and also ran countrywide fashion shows and 'Make and Measure' dress making competitions, in which every part of the garment from cloth to thread and buttons had to be of Irish manufacture. While production had to be verifiably local, NAIDA gave the operation international credibility by inviting overseas expertise, including the brilliant Italian designer, Elsa Schiaparelli to judge the fashions in the mid 1950s.[20] It was through NAIDA and Mrs O'Connor that Cleo came to supply the influential Irish-born and London-based designer, Digby Morton, a graduate of the Metropolitan School of Art (later the National College of Art & Design). Morton had 'established a reputation for impeccably tailored suits made in subtle, textured wools'[21] and, when in the mid 1950s he sought to add hand knitting to his collection he consulted NAIDA and Mrs O'Connor directed him to a reliable source, Kit Ryan in Cleo.

In turn Mrs Ryan went to her best knitters to fill this order, for what Kitty remembers as 'beautifully knitted full-length swinging coats'. One source was Mrs Ryan's nieces, highly skilled knitters from Hospital in Co. Limerick, with whom Kitty knit her first sweater, aged 9, while on summer holidays. For the Digby Morton coat (ill. p. 42), the Crowe nieces may have started with a pattern, but as they grew in familiarity and confidence with the design, Kitty feels it likely they will have added and subtracted from the original.

Digby Morton was not alone in seeking Irish wool. What the country offered in terms of tweeds and knits had been recently highlighted, through the fashion press, by the visit of the Philadelphia Fashion Group to Dublin in 1952. The benefit of this visit to celebrated designers, particularly Sybil Connolly and Irene Gilbert is well recorded,[22] but equally significant was the broader highlighting of Ireland, cloth and clothing, which profited tourism and trade – and Cleo. In the wake of this promotion even Christian Dior ordered knitwear from Cleo. Digby Morton was a significant designer in Britain and the United States but Christian Dior was arguably the dominant fashion force of the period. Kitty recalls with amusement how the occasional customer, dithering over whether or not to buy something, after spotting the Dior letterhead framed on the wall would decide to take two! However, Kitty equally remembers that it took forever to get paid by Dior. A young Irish girl studying French in Paris had to call eleven times, with invoices re-issued by Cleo, before the account was settled.

The card of Irish-born, London couturier, Digby Morton, stitched into the Cleo order book, c. May 1955.

CARMEL SNOW

Even those with little interest in fashion history are familiar with Dior's 'New Look'. His 1947 collection, rejecting wartime frugal functionality for overtly lavish fabrics and feminine shapes, was dubbed the 'New Look' by Carmel Snow, renowned fashion editor of *Harper's Bazaar*. The international impact of Snow's phrase is some indicator of her profound influence as editor of the fashion magazine from 1933 to 1957. Born in Dalkey, Co Dublin (1887), into a well-off Catholic family the New York based Carmel Snow returned to Ireland often and came into Cleo regularly, as Kitty remembers, always glamorously dressed. A vote of confidence in Cleo and a gesture that meant a great deal was Carmel Snow's featuring Cleo hand knits in *Harper's Bazaar* (c.1956, 1957).

Although the fashion endorsement of Carmel Snow might appear extremely remote from the Congested Districts Board promotions of Lady Aberdeen, they were in fact closely connected. In promoting Irish cloth and clothing Carmel

Overleaf: A Cleo order book of the 1950s is appropriately a rich collage of textures, colours, typefaces and handwriting.

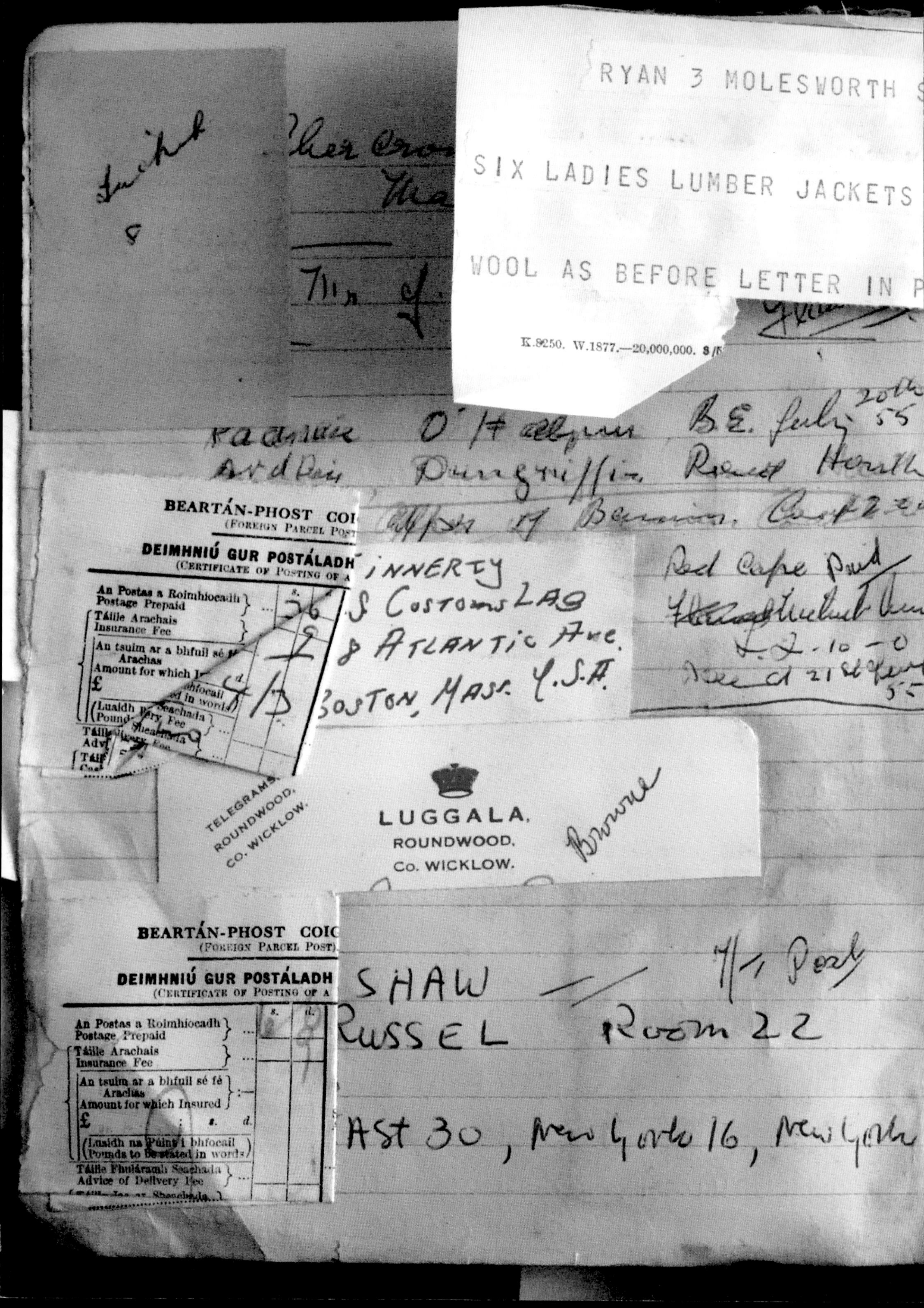

RYAN 3 MOLESWORTH S

SIX LADIES LUMBER JACKETS

WOOL AS BEFORE LETTER IN P

K.8250. W.1877.—20,000,000. 3/5

B.E. July 20th 55

Dungriffin Road Howth

Red Cape pnd

£2.10-0

55

BEARTÁN-PHOST COI
(FOREIGN PARCEL POST

DEIMHNIÚ GUR POSTÁLADH
(CERTIFICATE OF POSTING OF A

An Postas a Roimhiocadh
Postage Prepaid

Táille Arachais
Insurance Fee

An tsuim ar a bhfuil sé
Arachas
Amount for which I
£ d.

Luaidh na Púint i bhfocail
Pounds to be stated in words

Táille Fhuláramh Seachada
Advice of Delivery Fee

INNERTY
S CUSTOMS LAB
8 ATLANTIC AVE.
BOSTON, MASS. U.S.A.

TELEGRAMS
ROUNDWOOD,
CO. WICKLOW.

LUGGALA.
ROUNDWOOD.
Co. WICKLOW.

Browne

BEARTÁN-PHOST COIG
(FOREIGN PARCEL POST)

DEIMHNIÚ GUR POSTÁLADH
(CERTIFICATE OF POSTING OF A

An Postas a Roimhiocadh
Postage Prepaid

Táille Arachais
Insurance Fee

An tsuim ar a bhfuil sé fé
Arachas
Amount for which Insured
£ s. d.

Luaidh na Púint i bhfocail
Pounds to be stated in words

Táille Fhuláramh Seachada
Advice of Delivery Fee

SHAW
RUSSEL Room 22

AST 30, New York 16, New York

UBLIN =
E STYLE SIZE IN WASHED
= MORTON +
Mrs. Cyril J. Edwards
290 Provencal Road
Grosse Pointe Farms
Michigan
Caherciveen. Co. Kerry
be purchased or consulted at
any Post Office.
for Parcels only
Accepting Officer's Signature

Known in Cleo as the 'Kit Crowe Coat' (after its main knitter, the niece of Mrs Ryan) this handknit was produced in the mid 1950s for the London-based couturier Digby Morton. Representing 'London Fashion' in *Vogue* International Issue (15 September 1955) it featured as a double-page spread accompanied by the caption:

The apotheosis of the hand-knit. Roughly an elongated sweater cinched by a pigskin belt, it is one of several which Digby Morton has hand-knitted by women on the Isles of Aran in traditional stitch designs, and native, coarse unbleached wool. A Paisley cotton shirt fills the V neck. Pleated mustard felt beret by Rudolf.

Despite the romanticised identification of its maker as an islander, the style was in fact more often knit by, among others, Mrs Ryan's nieces in Co. Limerick.

Photograph: Condé Nast ltd – Eugene Vernier (Courtesy Trunk Archive).

In 1952 a group of American women involved in the fashion business, The Philadelphia Fashion Group, visited Dublin, with the assistance of CTT, the newly founded government agency aimed at developing and promoting Irish exports. Long recognised as a significant boost for signature Irish designers such as Sybil Connolly, this early success for CTT also saw the more anonymous, vernacular handweaves and handknits advanced by the group and Cleo, like others, benefitted from the exposure. The Philadelphia group also visited London where they were hosted at a garden party at the Hampstead home of Lady Kenneth Clark (President of the Incorporated Society of London Designers).

(Courtesy Mirror Pictures Archive).

Snow was continuing an endeavour pursued by both her parents in the late 19th century. Her father, Peter White, had worked for the Irish Woollen Manufacturing and Export Company in Dublin and had been asked by Lady Aberdeen to become honorary secretary of the Irish Industries Association. Together they worked on plans for the exhibition of Irish exports for the Irish Pavilion at the Chicago World's Fair (1893) and, according to an article in *The Citizen*, 'Ireland never selected a more fortunate representative than Mr Peter White. His amiable and sensitive manner wins confidence everywhere'.[23] However, Mr White's untimely death at the age of forty-three, just before the opening of The Chicago World's Fair, resulted in his wife taking over the enterprise – with such success that the Irish pavilion became the "hit of the fair".[24] Mrs White subsequently moved permanently to America, founding a fortune with The Irish Industrial Store, and from 1911 a custom dress-making establishment through which she became both rich and influential. Her daughter, Carmel, worked with her in the New York shop – not apparently with the same pleasure with which Kitty joined her mother – but even so the mother and daughter business in Cleo may also have struck a chord with Carmel Snow.[25] Snow's inclusion of Cleo knits in *Harper's Bazaar* was publicity many would have paid a great deal for and brought great custom to Cleo. When Mrs. Ryan asked her why she did it? Carmel Snow responded – 'Because you mind your business.'

Carmel Snow, editor-in-chief of *Harper's Bazaar* (1933-57) in conversation with couturier Balenciaga, December 1952. (Courtesy Getty Images)

CLEO CUSTOMERS

Along with such high profile clients Cleo's wider export trade also grew through the 1950s. The bulk of business however still came from visitors to Ireland and to a lesser extent from local custom, mainly from Dublin's well to do – or from the grander country houses – though these were of course in steep decline. Although fewer gentry and 'Colonels' ladies' continued to live fulltime in Ireland Cleo retained their established custom. For example the very earliest surviving record (8 January 1955) shows Lady Nelson, Co Wexford, placing a substantial order for:

5 Aran Island Jerseys at £4.4.0. each
1 crew neck at £3.10.0 1 red at £4.4.0
1 Aran Island paid for Red coat
4 jerseys paid for
Hats £7-14-0

The earliest surviving red order books record both the balance of business and the social geography of Cleo's earlier years. In 1955 custom from Ireland makes barely an impression and customers from Great Britain are almost matched by those from America. Perhaps surprisingly, the American names suggest no Irish roots, with a random selection including for example:

Mrs Franklin, Missouri, coat and stockings
Helen Emanuelson, Woodbridge, Connecticut
Constance Ohlsen, San Francisco, California
Miss J M Pipa, New York; 1 Man's coat, 'Devalue, Gift'
Louise Hendershot, Stockton, California
Terese David, Aspen Colorado, 1 coat, 2 Hats, 1 Balaclava, 2 Children's sweaters…
Miss King, Saxonia, Cunard Line, Sailing May 1st, Cobh, Cork
Mrs Neill Holloway, Montreal, Canada
Dr Rolfe Fogo, Fogo Island, Newfoundland, Canada.

From Britain, names include:
The Viscountess Bledisloe, Chelsea, London
The Earl of Weymouth, Wiltshire
Mrs Carter, Woodbine Cottage, Lincolnshire
Lady Sara Collins, Ayrshire, Scotland
Mrs Brown, Underwood Cottage, Berkshire
Mrs Brown, Portstewart, Northern Ireland

Among the few Irish customer names or addresses were:
Mr Vincent Gallagher, Gstaad, Switzerland
Mrs Benner, Tralee, Co Kerry

Of the Irish names that do appear it is clear the greater number are suppliers rather than customers of Cleo. Interspersed among customer names appear contact details for women living on the west coast of Ireland, who would knit the orders. Mrs Pat Flaherty on the Aran Islands, appears next to Mrs Guinness, Carton House, Maynooth. While historical and cultural analysis might separate the makers from the consumers of Irish clothing the Cleo order books are testament to their links

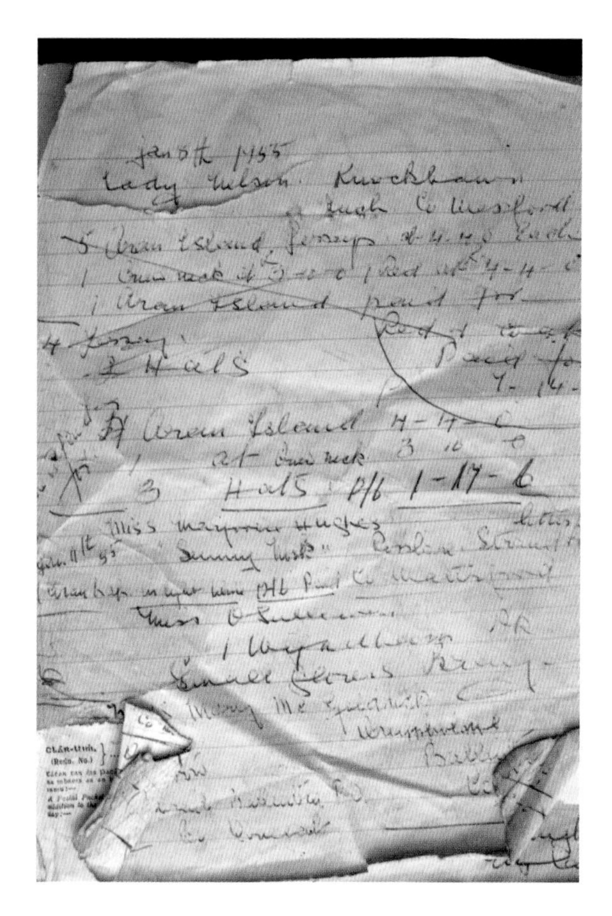

Lady Nelson Knockbawn

3 Hats

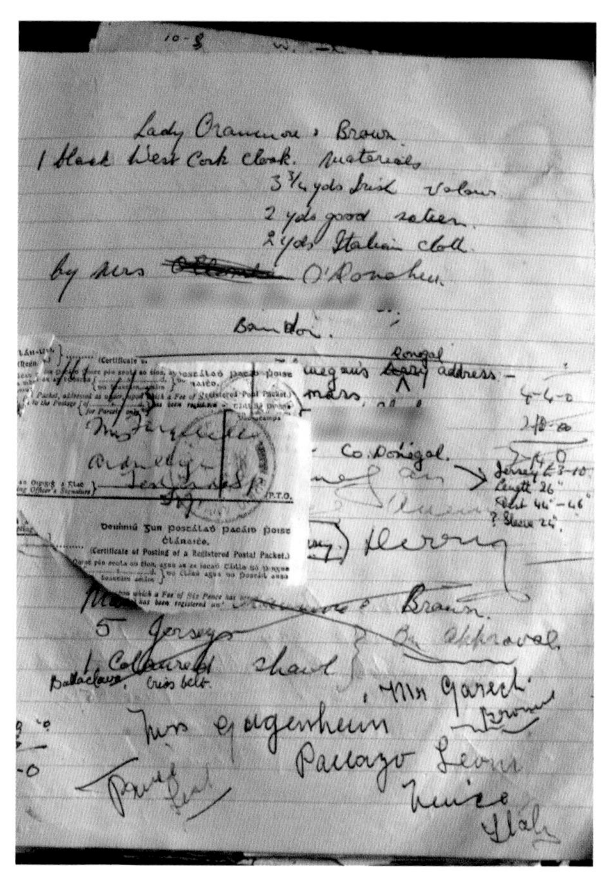

Lady Oranmore & Browne

1 Black West Cork Cloak. materials

3 1/4 yds Irish Velour

2 yds good sateen

2 yds Italian cloth

by Mrs O'Donohue

Bandon.

Co. Donegal.

Mrs Guggenheim

Palazzo Leoni

Venice

Italy

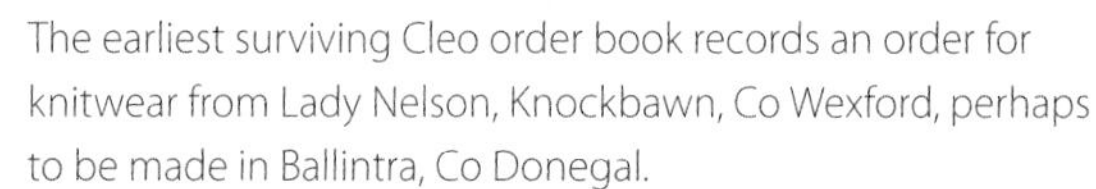

The earliest surviving Cleo order book records an order for knitwear from Lady Nelson, Knockbawn, Co Wexford, perhaps to be made in Ballintra, Co Donegal.

Lady Oranmore and Browne contributed greatly to the progress of Cleo, not only through her own custom but also through the many other people she and her family introduced to the shop – Peggy Guggenheim, for example, at Palazzo Leoni, in Venice.

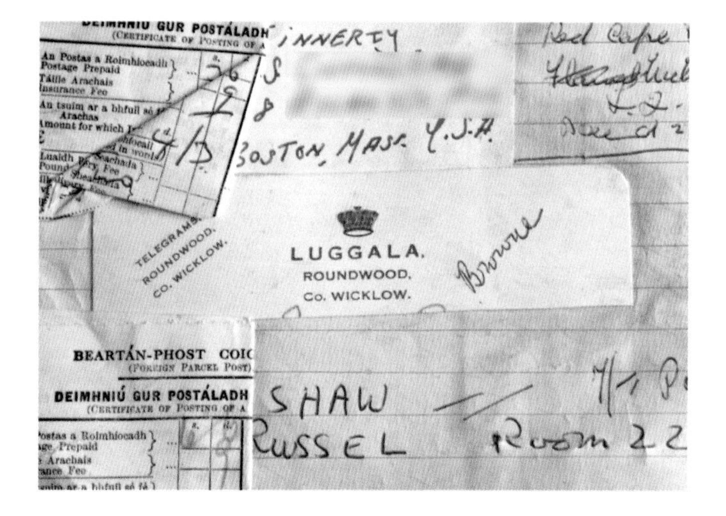

DEIMHNIÚ GUR POSTÁLADH

(CERTIFICATE OF POSTING OF A

Boston, Mass. U.S.A.

TELEGRAMS ROUNDWOOD. CO. WICKLOW.

LUGGALA. ROUNDWOOD. Co. WICKLOW.

Browne

BEARTÁN-PHOST COIC

(FOREIGN PARCEL POST)

DEIMHNIÚ GUR POSTÁLADH

SHAW

RUSSEL

Room 22

The contact details for Oranmore and Browne cut from their card and fixed into the order book for the purposes of communicating with Luggala, the hunting lodge inherited by Oonagh Guinness, where she lived in the Wicklow Mountains.

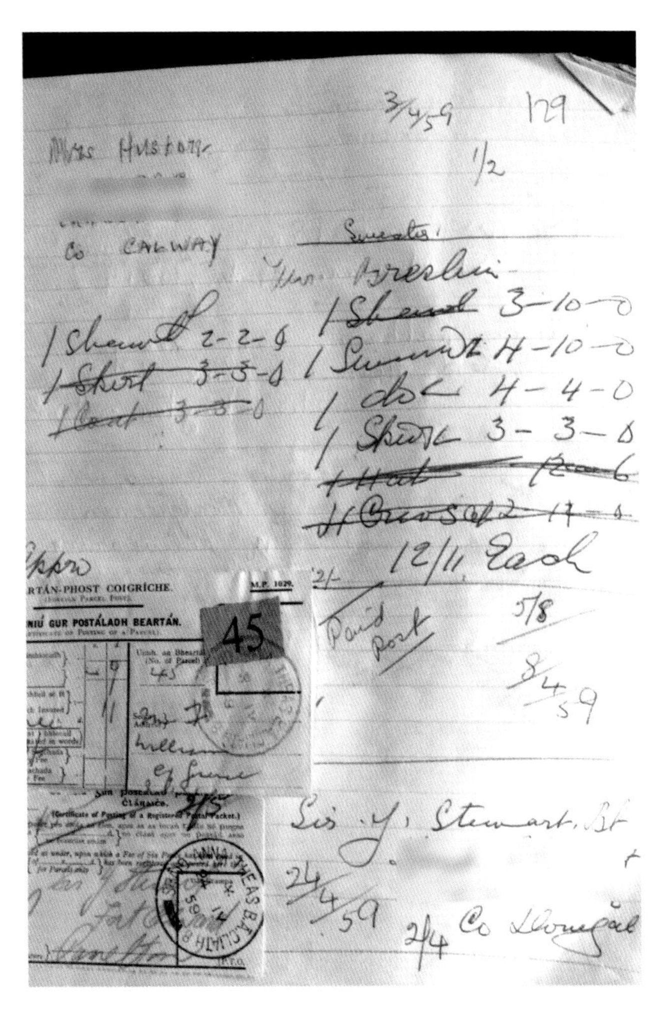
3/4/59 129
Mrs Huston
1/2
Co Galway
Sweater
Mrs Breslin
1 Shawl 3-10-0
1 Shawl 2-2-6
1 do 4-4-0
1 Skirt 3-3-6
12/11 Each
Paid post
5/8
8/4/59
RTÁN-PHOST COIGRÍCHE
M.P. 1029
NIÚ GUR POSTÁLADH BEARTÁN.
45
24/4/59
Co Donegal

The custom of Mrs Huston, St. Cleran's, Co Galway, had considerable impact on Cleo business in the 1950s and '60s and arguably still does.

Aran Coat. Miss Ria Mooney.
Abbey Theatre.
Bust 36"
Length 22". In oiley wool.
In May.

Another customer of Cleo was Ria Mooney (1904–73), artistic director of the Abbey Theatre 1948-63, and its first female producer. Kitty Joyce remembers her as 'a great dynamic woman who *was* the Abbey Theatre going to America'.

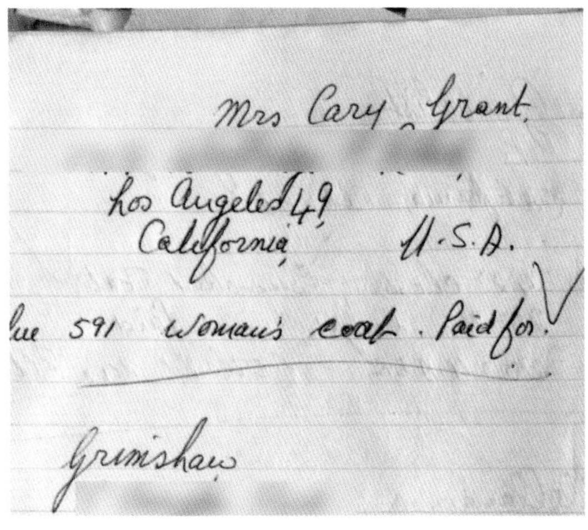
Mrs Cary Grant
Los Angeles 49
California U.S.A.
591 woman's coat. Paid for.
Grimshaw

Familiar names from literature, art and popular culture appear throughout the decades in Cleo's order books.

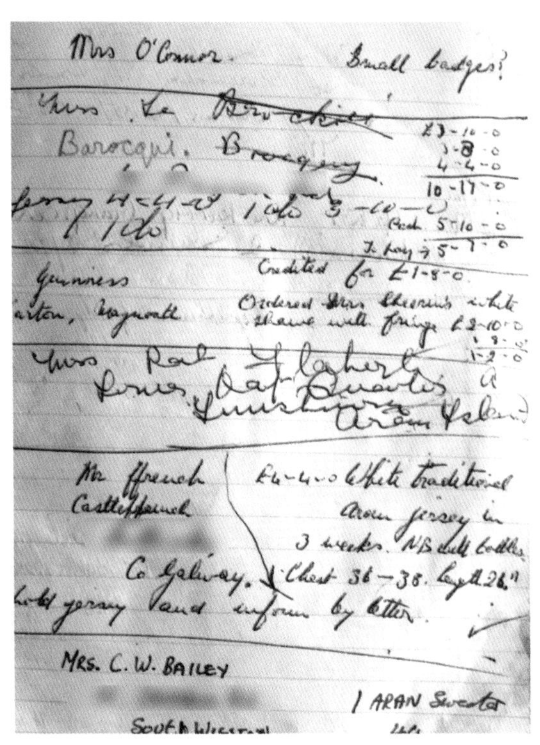
Mrs O'Connor. Small badges?
Mrs Le Brocki
Barocqui. Brockey
Guinness
Credited for £1-8-0
Mr ffrench
Castleffrench
Co Galway.
£4-4-0 White traditional Aran jersey in 3 weeks.
Chest 36-38. Length 26"
MRS. C. W. BAILEY
1 ARAN Sweater

An order was taken for Mr Paddy Collins, 30 Aughavana Road, Dolphin's Barn and another taken from, and a few attempts made to spell, Mrs Le Brocki, Barocqui, Brockey for 1 jersey.

and interrelationships. Names and addresses of makers and buyers appear side by side as they occur in the course of business, reflecting the discriminating but non-discriminatory philosophy of Cleo.

Lady Nelson of Co Wexford appears several times in the 1955 book. The most extensive custom, however, is from Lady Oranmore and Browne. Oranmore and Browne is a title from the West of Ireland, descending from one of the fourteen tribes of Galway, and Oonagh, Lady Oranmore was one of the three 'Golden Guinness Girls'. The Guinness and Oranmore taste for Irish names and Irish clothing suggests some declaration of pride in this distinguished lineage.

Just one example is an order from Lady Oranmore, before Christmas in 1955, that confirms her renowned commitment to Irish made clothing and explains her significance to Cleo. On this one visit she placed the substantial order; for her two sons:

3 tams, marron, make smaller, royal small size send
1 crios
1 £5-5-0 cable coat
1+1+1+2 pr gloves
2 jerseys to be paid for send bill

1 white for Master Oranmore Browne}
2 Polo to be washed } Post to Luggala
1 thin natural to be sent to England

SHANNON

However encouraging and prestigious this clientele, much of it represented a disappearing world and Cleo's growth would depend on wider custom from tourists, first from Britain and then beyond. Already with the opening of Shannon Airport in 1946 the number of North American tourists had begun to climb, supplementing the established visitor trade from Great Britain. Cleo's new location in Molesworth Street was ideal, directly opposite the Royal Hibernian Hotel where many visitors stayed. Business grew so briskly that Mrs Ryan was overwhelmed with customers, indeed this was largely what had prompted Kitty to leave nursing and commit full-time to the shop.

'Thank you for your time' the Americans would often say. This was something Cleo were not used to hearing and a concept they found amusing – 'we didn't notice our own time'. A less measured approach to life was perhaps part of what drew American tourists to Ireland after the War, as well as the much lower costs. Life in Ireland moved more slowly, and with less technology. It looked, and was, different to more modern American and European cities. Fashionable design in the 1950s, particularly in America, was based on mass-manufacture, plastics, chemicals and synthetic colours. The Americans who travelled were often looking for something different and were offered it in tourist posters encapsulating the West of Ireland as well as Hollywood depictions of the country.

By the time Cleo moved to Molesworth Street Hollywood had already produced compelling images of Ireland in Robert Flaherty's *Man of Aran* (1934) and John Ford would soon make *The Quiet Man* (1952). At the same time Aer Lingus and Bord Fáilte were developing a promotional image of the country for America and Europe with posters of fishermen of the West wearing hand knit and hand woven clothing. Thus invited to Ireland, tourists were prompted to see in the West an 'authenticity' missing from the modernity of their own ways of life, and to see in knitwear and weaving the embodiment of that 'authenticity'.[26]

Some visitors were taken enough with Ireland to stay. One particularly influential American artist, the film director John Huston, became an Irish citizen, and made the West his home for twenty years. He described Ireland as 'a jewel of a country – the bedrock of the world.' For Anjelica Huston, her father's identification with the country came from what he saw as its 'sense of freedom, of beauty, of poetry and daring'. She characterised 'his utter contempt for Beverly Hills' as a repudiation of 'everything that was fake and false and superficial and forgettable'. Her heartfelt account of his love for Ireland evokes how, by contrast, for him the country 'represented everything that was deep – and clear – and honest – and true... and beautiful'.[27]

Huston's wife Ricki quickly became a champion of Cleo's, as well as a stylish ambassador for their clothes. She also carried the image abroad, not only when she travelled, but also in selecting garments from Cleo for a boutique in Switzerland, run by an Irish friend. Skiing was a newly fashionable pursuit among the international jet set and their adoption of knitwear for the slopes gave it a youthful active glamour. As with golf wear in the 1930s, these new associations of moneyed independence broadened the appeal of knitwear and reinforced the interrelationship of wool, warmth, leisure and landscape.

Famously stylish and charming, Ricki Huston's recommendations carried weight, encouraging many from the movie business to visit Cleo in Molesworth Street. The names and addresses of those who had their tweeds and sweaters posted home remain in the red books, and among them many familiar names appear; Mrs Cary Grant, Mr Burgess Meredith and Mrs Dorothy Jeakins, the oscar-winning costume designer, who Kitty remembers as a 'very understanding and sympathetic person' and one of the first people to discover Cleo after the War.

One of Dorothy Jeakins' more significant orders was for Aran sweaters to be posted 'as soon a possible' to the 20th Century Fox Studios. The order came through Mr Edward McGuire, director of Brown Thomas Department store, who Kitty remembers coming in to Cleo around Christmas time, to report that a call had come through from Mrs Jeakins at three o'clock in the morning, asking him to go round to Cleo and order four identical Aran sweaters. With customary efficiency and no particular excitement Cleo had the 'jerseys' knit and posted, by special delivery service, from South Anne Street Post Office to Hollywood in late January 1960.The sweaters were needed for Marilyn Monroe to wear in the movie *Let's Make Love* released later that year, directed by George Cukor.

Looking back now, it might appear that Cleo had sought especially to cultivate an international clientele, from the creative to the aristocratic. In fact, this market had more or less created itself, by word of mouth, and with almost no advertising. For most Irish shoppers Cleo, though located at the heart of Dublin's best shopping district was, and remains, visible but unseen. A rare instance when the shop did advertise was precisely to try and entice some more Irish custom. In October 1956 Cleo placed an advertisement in the very first edition of *Creation*, Ireland's new 'Magazine of Fashion and Decor'.

ATTRACTING IRISH CUSTOM

In a section called 'Shopping Spree', Cleo knits appear in *Creation*, over several months, in small black and white images. Despite the copywriter's atttempts to associate the knits with high fashion, describing the colours as 'chic and sour', and drawing attention to Digby Morton's ordering his stock through Cleo, the promotion failed to attract the attention of the fashion-conscious Irish.

While *Creation* styled the images of Cleo clothes on fashionable models in contemporary poses and makeup, the knitwear still looked distinctly more handmade than the machine-knits appearing on other pages of the magazine. Cleo's handknits however will certainly have been warmer and longer lasting than much of the other knitwear advertised with blandishments such as:

> ' you're on the pedestal of fashion…in Siltona's new continentally-inspired, knitwear creation….Figure-flattering…alluring shades…exclusive pure Botany *Nylon* blends'.

Marilyn Monroe wore an Aran sweater in *Let's Make Love* (1960), costumed by Dorothy Jeakins, to whom four 'identical' sweaters were rushed from Cleo in January that year.

Cleo's advertisement had no discernable impact on sales, or even on interest shown in the shop, so *Creation's* fee of £3 seemed hard to justify – especially when £3 was a week's income for Mrs Ryan at the time. Other Irish clothiers advertising in the magazine must have had a similarly disappointing response given that the April 1957 edition carried an announcement:

> Wake up women of Ireland! Fashion is being born on your doorstep and you are passing it by. Clothes good enough for American and British girls are being spurned by our own women folk, and I simply do not know why. Shake off that grip of conservatism. Be bold. Wear vivid colours. Shocking pink or scarlet may not be out of place in your small home town.

'American and British girls' may have been more receptive to hand knitting as it was perhaps less familiar to them, and knitwear suited their casual, sporty, suburban style. But 'sporty suburbia' was not yet a widespread phenomenon in Ireland, where running water and electricty were still only being introduced to many households. A rather more 'respectable' suburbia becoming established, particularly in Dublin, was keen on escaping an impoverished past and all its associations.

For *Creation's* 'women of Ireland' hand knitting and hand weaving may have evoked embarrasing anxieties over status and modernity. Because home knitting remained a wardrobe staple for most Irish families, going to a shop to buy it at full price would be regarded, at best, as extravagant and, at worst, a sign of domestic inadequacy. Since the Famine, knitting helped dress Irish families and was pursued at home by mothers, sisters and grandmothers. Providing for the family's clothing needs contributed to a woman's status; if a mother did not herself knit she would usually have a female friend or relation to call upon, who would not expect payment at commercial rates. Knitwear therefore fell outside the normal commercial clothing system and was associated more with rural need than with urban desire.

Cleo's advertisement in *Creation* evoked a poignant memory for Brendan Behan, who published the following piece in a subsequent issue:

> Shawls
>
> I saw in a recent issue of *CREATION* that shawls "are fashion news again this year." The first shawl I had around me was a bright coloured Paisley the size of a tent. And that's not today nor yesterday, though I can still feel the warmth of the wool about me to this day. It contained two of us, my grandmother and myself.
>
> I was two years old or thereabouts, and though she was older she wasn't very big either, so there was plenty of room for the two of us…

Shopping

Traditional Aran Island sweater patterns now so popular in London high fashion. Digby Morton orders his through Cleo, Molesworth St., who stocks direct from the Aran Islands every sort of traditional hand-knitted garments. One item not otherwise found this side of Austria: men's extra-long bainin-wool golf stockings. The sweater, £4 4s. 0d. to £4 10s. 0d., depending on size.

To extend at home their success with visitors and international customers, Cleo advertised in Ireland's new glossy magazine Creation, appearing in the very first issue in 1956.

> Traditional Aran Island sweater patterns now so popular in London high fashion. Digby Morton orders his stock from Cleo, Molesworth Street, who stock direct from the Aran Islands every sort of traditional hand-knitted garments. One item not otherwise found this side of Austria: men's extra long bainin-wool golf stockings. The sweater £4. 4s.od. to £4. 10s. od. depending on size.

. . . in Siltona's new continentally
–inspired, knitwear creations . . .
Figure-flattering . . . alluring
shades . . . exclusive pure Botany
Nylon blends.

FASHION KNITWEAR

Shopping *SPREE*

Women all over Ireland will be glad when they hear that three Irish firms— Clarks Shoes, Beverly Bags and Horn Gloves—are co-operating so that the colours and textures of their materials will harmonise. When you buy a pair of Clarks shoes you will have absolutely no difficulty finding other accessories to tone or match them. Accordingly you will save yourself time and worry and perhaps be tempted to buy an unusual colour knowing that it can easily be matched. This sort of co-operation will help to make us more fashion and colour conscious. Above : A pair of sandals by Clarks. Available in black patent with transparent vamp and decorated Lucite heel.

At Cleo's, Molesworth Street, in wonderfully chic, sour colours, hand-knitted gloves and woolly hats in traditional patterns. Gloves, 11/6; capeen, 12/6.

The setting of this Cleo fashion shot, featured in *Creation*, reinforces the dual appeal of culture and nature in the shop. Harking back to the elegance and craftsmanship of 18th century Dublin, as did Cleo's location in Molesworth Street, the picture is set in the garden of a Georgian Square, and posed against the textured bark of a tree, emphasising the relationship between nature and handcraft.

With high production values *Creation* was a fashion and lifestyle magazine for Ireland, closely modelled on *Vogue*. The magazine ran from 1956 until the mid '60s.

> Arthur Miller's show followed mine in the Comedy Theatre and Marilyn was wearing a white shawl over her evening shoulders, so was Mrs Freddie Boland, and so was my wife Beatrice, all respectable married women of course, and entitled to wear them, though any one of their shawls was crepe suzette to a porterhouse steak compared to my granny's Paisley.
>
> She left it off once, when she was seventy, and bought a black hat and coat to go to Mass in, but coming down Gardiner Street, she met her older sister, who was very stern with her, and told her not to come out in a hat and coat any more." People will think you're. . .neither good nor middling," she muttered in a fierce whisper.
>
> Wistfully my granny put up her hat and coat, and after that only put them on in the house, to see herself in the mirror or ask me how she looked in them.[28]

Behan's vignette touches a nerve, and isolates the way social pressure to conform – to age or status – may be policed through clothing. For centuries the shawl had been the mark of a mature Irish woman (and a cloak its superior, more structured, sister). Only since the 1880s and '90s had a tailored coat, and hat, started to become the norm among young and progressive women. An elderly woman, like Behan's grandmother, wearing a coat and hat in the 1920s and even '30s, might be regarded as aspiring to youth, status or modernity – any one of which appears to have been mortifying to the older sister in the story.

Opposite: *Creation* Oct. 1956 Vol. 1 No. 1. In 1956 the contrast between machine knits and hand knits is palpable in the pages of *Creation*. The smooth mass produced 'product', it seems, found greater favour with middle-class Irish shoppers, than did the familiar texture and individuality of hand knitting.

The Irish playwright Sean O'Casey in a very finely knit Aran sweater, several of which were ordered from Cleo by his wife, Eileen. (Courtesy Getty Images)

Those Irish who did patronise Cleo, including as it happens, Brendan Behan and his wife Beatrice, tended to be artistic or literary. Familiar names placing orders through 1956-7 included the playwright's wife Mrs Sean O'Casey, who along with her family were regular customers, and Mrs Walsh, [the writer, Mary Lavin], Bective, Co Meath who ordered what is described as a 'priest's aran sweater' suggesting the knitter would know herself the specific requirements for a priest. Another was the Hon John ffrench, with an address at The Ring Ceramic Studio, who was, like Browne, from an old Irish family, also one of the tribes of Galway.

Unlike the middle-classes, Irish artists and writers of the mid century, appear to have identified to some extent with Cleo or at least with the Aran sweater, perhaps for several reasons, including as a means of distancing themselves from conformist middle-class values and in opposition to the shirt and tie of the bureaucrat. For some, like Patrick Kavanagh, the hand knit sweater will have been a vital weapon in his armoury against cold flats around Baggot Street. For many the knitted sweater and cap was the latest in a long history of what might be termed 'contemplative wear' worn to provide warmth and physical ease while pursuing sedentary work. In Ireland, and among the creative Irish, the Aran sweater was perhaps chosen, as a form of identification with what might be regarded as a 'national spirit'.

Endnotes

1 Usher, R. (2008) *Dawson, Molesworth & Kildare Streets D2*, Dublin Civic Trust, cover.

2 Ibid. p. 44.

3 *Thom's Directory* (1955) p.1061.

4 O'Kelly, Hilary in conversation with her in-law Josephine Gallagher Co Donegal. The perceptive question was asked by Oscar O'Mahoney, Co. Cork.

5 O'Kelly, Hilary, ibid.

6 Beattie, Sean, *Donegal Annual 2009*, 'Cottage Industries: Arts and Crafts in Donegal 1810–1920' www.historyofdonegal.com/DonegalAnnual09_seans.pdf.

7 Adamson, Glenn (2007) *Thinking Through Craft*, Oxford, Berg, p. 69.

8 Turney, Joanne (2009) *The Culture of Knitting*, Oxford, Berg, p. 66.

9 For a discussion see Adamson, Glenn op cit. pp.105-6.

10 Synge, J.M. (1907) *The Aran Islands*. With thanks to Dr. Lisa Godson for this reference.

11 Turney, Joanne, op cit. p. 47.

12 Adamson, Glenn, op cit. p. 104.

13 Turney, Joanne, op cit. p. 48.

14 O'Kelly, Hilary (02 March 2013) in phone conversation with Betty Hewitt, Dublin, who knit for Cleo in the 1980s and '90s.

15 Nuttall Sayres, Meghan (Autumn 2001) *New Hibernia Review*, 'Conversations in Donegal: Mary McNelis and Con O'Gara', p. 12.

16 For the best discussion on Aran sweaters see Deirdre McQuillan, (1993) *The Aran Sweater*, Belfast, Appletree Press.

17 'Fabric shoppers' Paradise, Tea, Cookies and Fine Tweeds At the End of Carol Brown's Putney Rainbow' an unidentified newspaper article in the Cleo archive NIVAL, The National Irish Visual Arts Library, The National College of Art & Design.

18 Ryan, Vera (2006) *Movers & Shapers 2, Irish Visual Art 1940–2006*, Cork, Collins Press, p. 15.

19 Daly, Mary E. (1992) *Industrial Development and Irish National Identity, 1922–1939*, Gill and Macmillan, Dublin, p. 43.

20 See Clery, Elizabeth (2003) *Néillí Mulcahy Couturière 1951–1969*, Unpublished MA thesis NCAD p. 100

21 de la Haye, Amy and V. Mendes (1999) *Twentieth Century Fashion*, London, Thames & Hudson, p.76.

22 McCrum, E. (1996) *Fabric and Form: Irish Fashion Since 1950*, p.16 and O'Byrne, R. (2000) *After a Fashion, a history of the Irish fashion industry*, p.29.

23 Rowlands, Penelope, 2005, *A Dash of Daring, Carmel Snow and her Life in Fashion, Art, and Letters*, New York, Atria Books, pp. 6-8.

24 Ibid. p. 13.

25 Ibid, p. 31.

26 As discussed by Linda King (2011) in '(De) constructing the Tourist Gaze: Dutch Influences and Aer Lingus Tourism Posters, 1950–1960'. In King, Linda and Elaine Sisson, *Ireland, Design and Visual Culture: negotiating Modernity, 1922–1992*, Cork, Cork University Press.

27 Roper, Anne (2009) An American in Galway, RTÉ.

28 *Creation*, January 1957, Vol. 2 No. 1.

BLACKBERRY & POPCORN

Tradition and Modernity

BUSINESS

Garment by garment and order by order, looking after the precise quality of their 'wearable art' and the particular needs of the individual customer is indeed, as Carmel Snow observed, what Cleo has done since the earliest days. Although not a bespoke business Cleo's personalised way of bringing together the maker and buyer evolved in opposition to business models developing alongside mass manufacture and mass consumption. Driven by war-time innovation, the post-war period saw dramatic development in materials, fabrication, markets and

Cleo's years in Molesworth Street (c.1950-1973) spanned a period of transition in Ireland, often characterised as 'from tradition to modernity'. In this Cleo image both are evident; the Aran stitch and hay bales obviously connecting with older Ireland, but in colour and form the knitwear and weaving belong to the mid 20th century (c. 1970) as does the diverse range of clothing options and the suggestion of women's increasing adoption of trousers. (Photo Bill Doyle. Models; friends and relations of the photographer)

marketing, mirroring a new fast-paced, car-based suburban living. Originating in America, this new lifestyle was known even to people who had not experienced it themselves, through films and later television. Business too changed rapidly. Many firms surviving the war evolved in tandem with these mass-market values, while others were born out of the new landscape. In Ireland, government policy would increasingly see the future in large-scale, mass-market production and export. Cleo's ethos however, belongs to an older more personal notion of business, and has remained focused on the individual, the hand made, the one-off and small-scale manufacture. From its produce to its location Cleo's touchstone – even as it changes – has been continuity rather than reaction to fashions or politics. Government strategy on the other hand declared a vision for the future based on replacing the old with the new. New economic and political strategies now focused Ireland outwards towards Europe and America rather than inwards. Perhaps throwing the baby, its unique heritage, out with the bathwater, self-sufficiency.

Despite these wider changes trading remained familiar territory for Cleo until the mid 1960s. Prices were strong, there was no inflation, and the Trade Board (Córas Tráchtála Teoranta, est. 1952) had not yet effected change in the nature of doing business in Ireland. But from the mid '60s Kitty recalls new business courses being established and with them came a debilitating increase in layers of bureaucracy, what she calls the 'treacle effect'. The simplicity of trade was disappearing. Certainly the surviving Cleo pen and ink account books from the 1950s reflect a modest and straightforward approach to business and expenditure under headings such as: 'Stationary', 'Stock', 'Advertising', 'Post', 'Rent', 'Salary', and 'Bags of twine.' Compared with recent years of prosperity in Ireland, when office workers hired motor-cycle couriers to pick up their cappuccino from a café down the road, Cleo's discretionary expenses and personal outgoings also record a simpler time with week after week nothing being spent beyond: 'Rent', 'Rent Rathmines', 'Insurance', 'Food', 'Mass-Offerings', 'Housekeeping', 'E.S.B.' 'Charity', regular trips to the chiropodist, the occasional purchase of a hat, coat or wedding present and a rare taxi fare.

From 1956, the Cleo pen and ink records began to be written in biro, an instrument, Kitty recalls, a superior in school insisting 'the banks would never accept!' But shortly all hand-written financial summaries were replaced by the accountant Cleo was instructed to employ:

> By 1960 Ireland's economy had begun to improve, and there were many concomitant social changes... Business and marketing became more professional and educational standards improved drastically. The setting up of Kilkenny Design Workshops in 1964 at the instigation of Córas Tráchtála revolutionised public awareness of design... The advent of national television in 1962 and increasingly effective marketing by Bord Fáilte brought the world to Ireland, and Ireland to the world. Ireland was becoming more outward looking and international in attitude – just as the new tourist industry was extolling its pre-industrial and unchanging charms.[1]

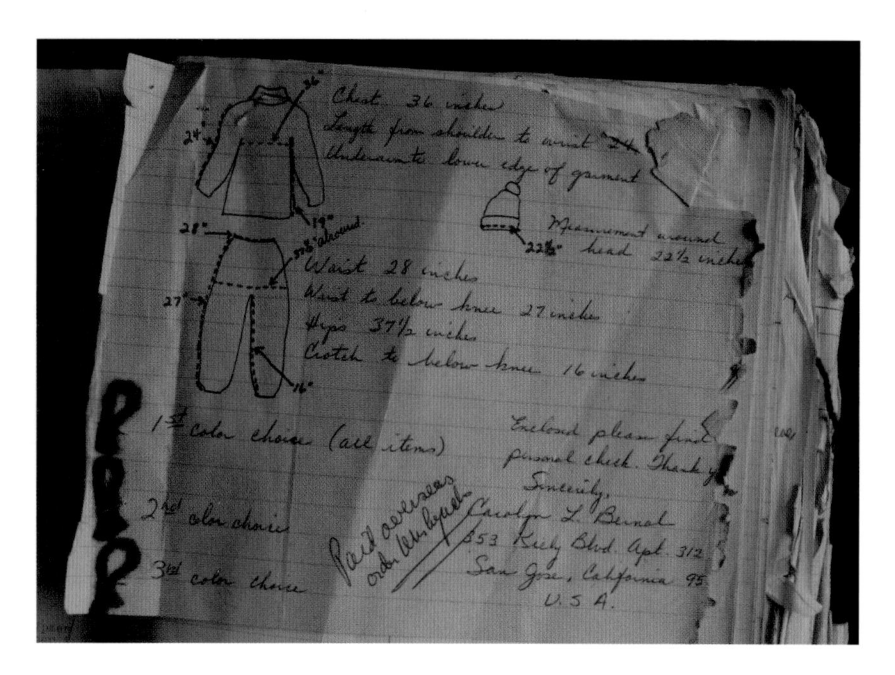

Chest 36 inches
Length from shoulder to wrist 24
Underarm to lower edge of garment
Measurement around head 22½ inches
Waist 28 inches
Waist to below knee 27 inches
Hips 37½ inches
Crotch to below knee 16 inches
1st color choice (all items)
2nd color choice
3rd color choice
Enclosed please find personal check. Thank you
Sincerely,
Carolyn L. Bernal
353 Kiely Blvd. Apt. 312
San Jose, California 95
U.S.A.
Paid overseas order

The decline of personal interaction in business, to be replaced by increasingly bureaucratic modes, is reflected in two customer orders appearing on consecutive pages of a Cleo order book. In one a customer requests a knitted ski outfit, described by her own drawing and measurements, and including alternative colour preferences (allowing for availability) suggesting she had a good understanding of what was involved in the supply of a hand made outfit.

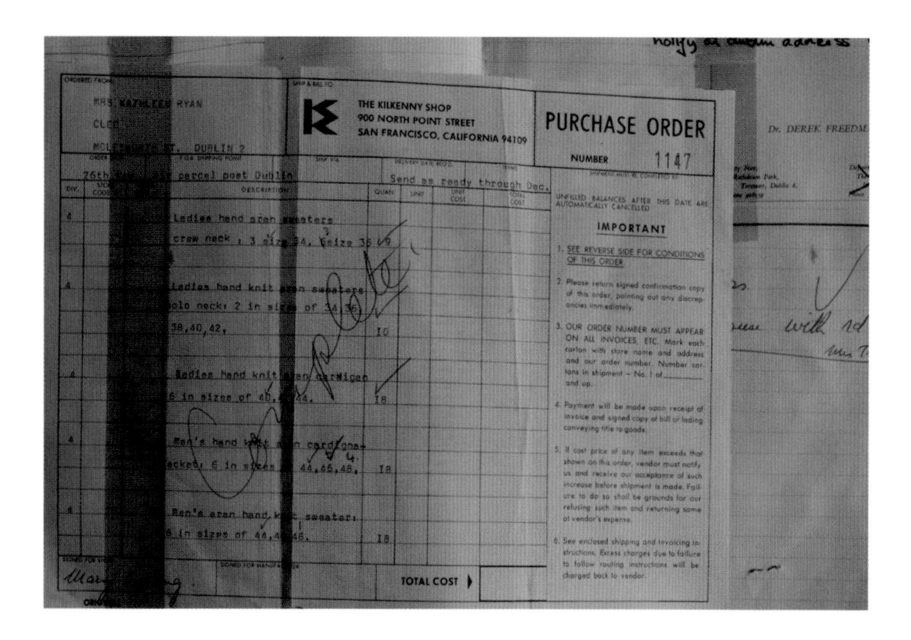

THE KILKENNY SHOP
900 NORTH POINT STREET
SAN FRANCISCO, CALIFORNIA 94109

PURCHASE ORDER
NUMBER 1147

MRS. KATHLEEN RYAN
CLEO
MOLESWORTH ST. DUBLIN 2

26th ... parcel post Dublin
Send as ready through Dec.

DIV.	DESCRIPTION	QUAN.
4	Ladies hand aran sweaters crew neck ; 3 size 34, 3 size 36	
4	Ladies hand knit aran sweaters polo neck: 2 in sizes of 34,36, 38,40,42,	10
4	Ladies hand knit aran cardigan 6 in sizes of 40,42,44.	18
4	Men's hand knit aran cardigan jackets: 6 in sizes 44,46,48,	18
4	Men's aran hand knit sweater: 6 in sizes of 44,46,48.	18

TOTAL COST

UNFILLED BALANCES AFTER THIS DATE ARE AUTOMATICALLY CANCELLED

IMPORTANT

1. SEE REVERSE SIDE FOR CONDITIONS OF THIS ORDER
2. Please return signed confirmation copy of this order, pointing out any discrepancies immediately.
3. OUR ORDER NUMBER MUST APPEAR ON ALL INVOICES, ETC. Mark each carton with store name and address and our order number. Number cartons in shipment – No. 1 of ____ and up.
4. Payment will be made upon receipt of invoice and signed copy of bill of lading conveying title to goods.
5. If cost price of any item exceeds that shown on this order, vendor must notify us and receive our acceptance of such increase before shipment is made. Failure to do so shall be grounds for our refusing such item and returning same at vendor's expense.
6. See enclosed shipping and invoicing instructions. Excess charges due to failure to follow routing instructions will be charged back to vendor.

By contrast this Kilkenny Design document records an order for multiple hand-made sweaters in standardized manufacturing sizes. The order form stipulates the garments are to be delivered on specific dates, with failure to comply resulting in non-payment of the account. Such a cut-and-dried approach towards a craft enterprise like Cleo may have contributed to provoking the peaceable Carol Brown, importer of Irish goods to North America since the 1920s, to bang her fist on the table during a meeting with them – declaring 'I HATE Kilkenny Design!'

Cleo's world of craft and manufacture saw many changes in systems and attitudes following from the T.K.Whittaker economic expansion programme (1958), the 'Scandinavian Report' (1962) and the setting up of Kilkenny Design Workshops (1963).[2] Expansion programmes increased trade and employment, but, as Kitty saw it, the human dimension of trading and customer interaction was being eroded. For years Cleo business communications had been typified by Carol Brown's quirky letters or dispatches from overseas-customers placing individual orders and including drawings and personal details. Now increasingly these were replaced by official order forms and accounting requirements to issue documents in triplicate.

FASHION

Meanwhile, as Cleo continued to work with one-off or small-order makers of unique garments and cloths of local material and design, Irish trade policy saw mass production and volume sales of fashion as the future for Ireland. At the same time, however, the international fashion world essentially retained its image of Ireland as a place of timeless quality rather than up-to-the minute style. Cleo, though nurturing this very produce for which Ireland is known abroad, did not feel government trade initiatives valued their contribution. As Kitty saw it, it was 'quite the opposite' so it was both amusing and gratifying when Cleo's work found favour in unexpected quarters.

In November 1971 Córas Tráchtála [CTT] invited the Paris designer André Courrèges, to Dublin. Described in the international press as the 'Le Corbusier of fashion,'[3] the Trade Board had asked him to address a seminar of designers and manufacturers at the RDS. As CTT were looking to Courrèges, known particularly for his 'Space-Age' designs, to advise the Irish clothing industry, it is perhaps not surprising that, at the same time, Kitty felt they were rather dismissive towards Cleo. Nevertheless Kitty decided to attend the seminar, leaving the shop in the hands of Catherine Tobin, a long time friend and creative collaborator of Cleo. As Kitty was leaving the shop to go to the RDS 'Catherine was looking after a funny little man in a white suit' – when Kitty reached the RDS she realised 'the little man' was Courrèges. In an interview in *The Irish Independent* it was reported that Courrèges 'was disappointed with the clothes in Irish shops. A quick guided tour of Grafton Street (his pale blue ciré suit must have caused a stir), had, he said revealed little of interest – except those sweaters and rain coats.'[4]

THE SCANDINAVIAN REPORT

Negotiating a relationship between tradition and modernity formed part of every aspect of Irish life in the middle of the 20th century; in social norms, economic policies and religious beliefs transitions were forged in theory and in practice. In terms of craft, design and manufacture the great attempt to allign tradition and modernity in Ireland was the Kilkenny Design Workshop. Established through the mid 1960s, its aim was to develop modern exports based on Ireland's native resources and skills. It was set up not necessarily because of, but in the aftermath of, the report popularly known as the 'Scandinavian Report' of 1962.[5] One aim of inviting Scandinavian designers to Ireland had been to identify strengths and weaknesses of Irish design and manufacture with a view to developing government policy in the area of export.

As the Scandinavian evaluation was commissioned by CTT, a particular aim was to strengthen the economy through successful export of well-designed goods. Although Cleo was not involved in any way with the Scandinavian visit or report, the conclusions drawn nonetheless coincided with the Cleo view. Identified as among the greatest strengths of Irish design were Donegal tweed and Irish hand knitting. Among the greatest weaknesses isolated were 'woollen and other woven cloth, where the influence from abroad is nowhere more evident' than in:

> firms set up to replace imported textile goods and protected against their competition. We feel that many of the faults to be found in Irish textiles spring from this cause.
>
> Because they are attempting to replace the foreign-manufactured article they have tried to imitate it and manufacture a great many lines with a mixture of foreign styles and production techniques. Instead of being Irish, their textile goods are French, English or Japanese, and we know from our experience that this is a disastrous approach.[6]

The report highlighted particular qualities that distinguished the good from the bad:

> The original tweeds ... derive their effect from a connection with nature and ... we must advise you to take care of this line of production and pay attention to good materials, careful craftsmanship and practical form.[7]

The views of the Scandinavian group mirrored a growing international interest in small-scale craft production. The tourism industry capitalised on this perspective and projected the image of Ireland as a 'pre-industrial' society. The government however seems to have had difficulty relating craft with modernity and particularly in locating the role of the individual craftsperson in the development of the Irish economy. Something of the government's uncertainty over how to relate to craft, and of its relationship to the economy and culture, is signalled by the variety of government authorities under which it has been placed. Craft and design first came under the auspices of the Department of Industry and Agriculture, and NAIDA, in the 1920s and 30s. By 1951 The Arts Council had jurisdiction over craft, in 1960 it came under the Trade Board, and in 1971 the Crafts Council, which was established and funded by the Department of Trade, Enterprise and Employment. Government interest in Ireland's craft base has appeared aimed at large scale manufacture, volume employment and expanding exports. But it is difficult to foster volume production while at the same time nurturing individual creativity, particularly if using shared promotional institutions and marketing methods.

Perhaps it has been a mismatch of scale that has led to Cleo's sense of being outside government schemes for promoting craft. While the government looked to potential new models, Cleo looked to supporting and building on what already existed in the country.

CLEO CLOTHING & KNITWEAR

Cleo constantly sought out small scale producers to supply the shop, and by the early 1970s had widened their clothing range to include fisherman's trousers, of the sort worn on Aran, made in wool and later linen, with a high waist and buttoned front.

Kitty had a version made up by the tailor Austin Lendaro, in Dublin. Perhaps the success of these warm, comfortable and distinctive trousers among a metropolitan clientele was helped by the film, *Ryan's Daughter* (1970) which romanticised the

A Cleo Aran waistcoat (top right), produced by a Dublin tailor, pictured c.1970. Sourcing handmade goods from rural Ireland became increasingly difficult in the 1960s and '70s – sometimes even when the skills and materials were still available. Models: friends and relations of photographer Bill Doyle and Cleo, with Brenda Smyth (centre), Cleo's first employee.

ARAN HAND KNITTERS REQUIRED

CONSTANT WORK, FOR KNITTING MAN'S BUTTONED JACKET £3.90
MAN'S PULLOVER £3.60. WOMAN'S PULLOVER £3.30
WOMAN'S BUTTONED JACKET £3.60
SEND SAMPLE (which need not be new), Pullover or Cardigan with sleeves to:
CLEO LTD., No. 3 Molesworth St., DUBLIN 2.
ENCLOSING NAME AND ADDRESS. MARK PACKAGE "SAMPLE"

A Cleo call for knitters (archive cutting: news on the verso indicates the paper was local to South Donegal). Publishing a price scale suggests Cleo fees were competitive with the going rate. At the time Cleo wholesale price per garment was twice what was paid to the knitter, ie:
Man's buttoned jacket £3.60 to knitter £7.10 wholesale
Man's Pullover £3.60 to knitter £7.00 wholesale
Woman's buttoned jacket £3.60 to knitter £6.10 wholesale

western seaboard of Ireland. It may also have been helped by the 1970s revival of the styles of the 1920s and '30s seen in other films like *The Great Gatsby* (1974) and *Annie Hall* (1977) which featured women wearing over-sized men's clothes. Later Cleo added another garment of fisherman origin, an Aran waistcoat in tweed, lined with a lighter layer of wool at the chest (originally to protect fishermen from oncoming winds). Here again the garment was made up in Dublin by Austin Lendaro, as the western tailor couldn't be persuaded to supply the waistcoat for fear that taking commercial orders would threaten his dole allowance.

The reliability of a state income-support, versus the risk of uncertain orders for garments, is just one example of how new structures were making handcraft less viable as a realistic livelihood. What was once seen as a valuable addition to household income now looked like pin-money, resulting in a dwindling of craft skills. The search for skilled knitters has therefore occupied Cleo throughout their years in business. On many occasions Mrs Ryan or Kitty travelled to rural Ireland to look for knitters, but when they couldn't they advertised in rural papers or women's magazines. In the early '70s Cleo returned to South Donegal, where they had success in the 1950s, and advertised in a paper local to Ballintra.

When Cleo had first begun to sell knitwear, in the 1940s, skilled knitters were plentiful. But by the 1960s and '70s their numbers were in steep decline. By then the first knitters were growing older, and young women continued to emigrate, or if at home, increasingly in paid employment or simply not interested or skilled in knitting. In 1966 Cleo wrote to *Woman's Way* the Irish weekly magazine, to put out a call for knitters. But as it turned out this proved unnecessary, as the magazine already had a list of knitters who had independently contacted the magazine looking for suggestions for knitting work.

In an attempt to find a more concentrated group of knitters, in the changing world of the mid-century, Kitty and Marie Murtagh, her old school-friend now working in Cleo, went door to door in the recently built suburb of Tallaght, but a concentration of knitters were not to be found there. Whenever possible, new skills are added to their established knitters, many of whom are the children and grand children of the original women.

WEAVING

Cleo stock has always included hand-made clothing in Irish woven cloth, often handwoven. But hand weaving, like knitting skills were in decline, and even weaving mills closed as the Irish weaving industry fell to international competition. Working with weavers on a less industrial scale helped Cleo offer

woman's way  ireland's national magazine for women

Knit. Ed.
Woman's Way
23 Grafton Street
Dublin 2
15.8.66

Mrs. Ryan,
Cleo, 3 Molesworth Street,
Dublin.

Dear Mrs. Ryan,

Thank you for letter. Several ladies have written to me asking to be put in contact with firms who employ good Aran knitters. I have given the names of firms but I fear they may be full up and unable to take on more knitters so I'm delighted to know you can absorb some. In future may I give your name and address to ladies who write re Aran knitting and on the back of this letter I will give you a few names and addresses of readers who wrote to me recently and who may be disappointed as regards other firms

Yours sincerely

Moira

advertising offices: creat

Mrs Lignagappul, Annascaul, Kerry ✓
Miss Blackhall, Abbeyleix via Portlaoise ✓
Mrs White Hall, Kilcullen, Co. Kildare ✓
Mrs Main Street, Edgeworthstown, Co. Longford. ✓
Mrs Chapel Road, Kilronan, Aran Isles
4 Killarney Ctgs. Kenmare, Co. Kerry ✓
Miss Quin, Ennis, Co. Clare ✓
Mrs. Bishopsland, Kildare ✓
Mrs. Beaghmore, Ballinasloe, Galway ✓
Mrs St. Margaret's, Rosslare Strand, Co Wexford.
Mrs Main Street, St. Johnston, Lifford, Co. Donegal. ✓
Mrs Bank Place, Ennis, Co. Clare ✓
Mrs. Eden Road, Birr, Offaly. ✓

I know nothing at all about the quality of the knitting of course and I cannot give you any references re the ladies.

Where earlier, skilled knitters had been plentiful, by 1966 this civil and careful correspondence between *Woman's Way* and Cleo suggests knitters were no longer to be found in small rural pockets. Instead, to source a range of knitting skills it was necessary to trawl the whole country, from Kerry to Donegal and Clare to Kildare, though no knitter in Dublin appears here.

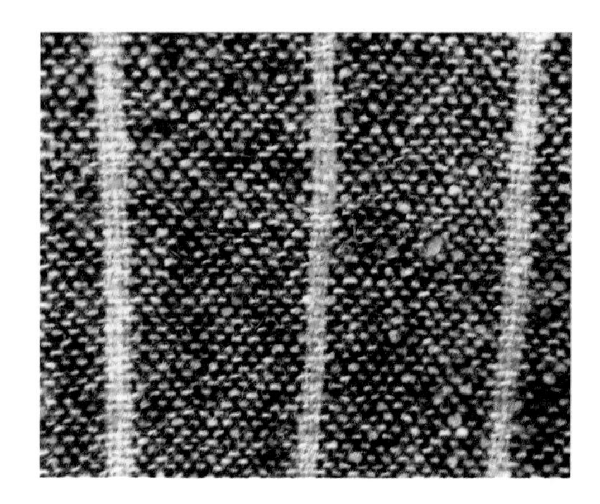

A soft wool cloth handwoven by Marianne Lavelle, and made into a silk-lined jacket for Cleo.

fabrics and tweeds with more personality and individuality than their industrial counterparts. Subtlety and variation in colour and texture are part of what makes tweed such a compelling fabric. It is not simply by happy accident these qualities are achieved but by sensitive and experienced decision-making.

Colour is of great importance to Cleo. Although their banner 'handknits and handweaves' might well suggest an emporium of creams and browns with touches of heather, a defining quality of their knits and weaves has always been the richness of singing colour. Achieving this range is a priority for Cleo and their work in promoting quality weaving is appreciated by the mills and hand weavers surviving around the country. Michael Molloy, of Ardara weavers John Molloy, claims Kitty Joyce has been of great importance to Irish weaving but is little recognised.[8]

Commissioning handwoven, or even machine woven, cloth for commercial ends is an involved process, and not for the faint-hearted. When dealing in small runs of cloth achieving a reliable supply and a consistency of standard is not an easy or exact science, with variations occurring not only in colour but also in texture and the 'handle' of the fabric. One correspondence surviving in the archive suggests the commitment required to achieve a desired quality and can be followed in negotiations over the subtleties of a bolt of blue cloth ordered from the Gaeltarra Éireann mills, 'Connemara Fabrics' (in Kilcar, Co. Donegal).

Having exhausted an earlier length of this blue wool fabric Cleo ordered a further bolt which was delivered over Christmas 1980. In Cleo's view it was an unsatisfactory replacement for the original, and they had Connemara Fabrics collect it from Dublin to be re-dyed in Donegal. At first glance the samples might seem hardly distinguishable. However, under the guidance of Cleo, what becomes evident is the soft rich subtlety of the original weave (A) against the harsher colour of the replacement cloth (B) and, in the redyed cloth (C), though the colour has been improved its texture remains more lifeless and flat.

When dealing with a smaller-scale hand weaver sustained discussion between maker and client, about colour, texture and pattern, constituted part of the design process. One such producer was Noirín Kennedy of The Weaver's Shed whose work impressed Cleo greatly. She had learnt her skills in Donegal with weavers whom she described designing cloth as they made it, selecting colours and textures from a palette of wools spread out around their workshop.[9] The close working relationship and understanding between Cleo and The Weaver's Shed is evident in a letter reaffirming a conversation that had taken place in Noirín Kennedy's Kilmainham Mills. In the letter Noirín's brother, Loughlin Kennedy, reiterates Kitty's order for fabrics including:

> 80 yards of the funny tweed in blues and greys with a little brown: We are to weave it keeping the bands irregular – based on the artistic inspiration of an experienced weaver! ... Funny tweed in reddish-brown: . . .We could make it a little wilder in design - sample a bit too rigid, too much like a plaid; crossbars could be more uneven or perhaps have the edges softened by a transition colour.

Sample swatches from Connemara Fabrics Ltd. (Co. Donegal) for evaluation by Cleo. Though to the untrained eye the fabrics may appear closely alike, their slight differences consumed much time and expense.

This fastidious sensitivity to quality, lavished on each piece of Cleo stock, was not matched by the majority of produce supplying the tourist trade. Kitty recalls the 1970s when *crios* belts from the Aran Islands arrived in Cleo made from rough shop-bought wools glaringly dyed in *red! blue!* and *green!* In an attempt to bring her *crios* range up to the standard of the rest of Cleo she enrolled on a weaving course, run by Lillias Mitchell, in The National College of Art & Design, to learn the skill herself. The project was short lived, however, ending when she came upon a skilled weaver in Northern Ireland, for whom she sourced softer shades of wool in better quality to weave the narrow belts, valued as much to warm the vital organs as a means of supporting the trousers.

A crios belt, native to the Aran Islands, originally woven without a loom. (Courtesy Cleo)

CRAFT

Such carefully considered goods require customers who recognise and value the difference. That appreciation is not necessarily constant, but moves across the globe as wider circumstances change, from place to place and group to group. Already by the mid-19th century an identification of the merits of craft in comparison with mass manufacture went hand-in-hand with industrialisation. The cultural debate was perhaps first framed and best advanced in the work of John Ruskin and William Morris. One hundred years later, in the post-war world, a renewed appreciation of artisan craft production was becoming well established among the socially and politically disillusioned. Equally, the material beauty as well as the social merit of craft work was finding recognition and a consumer base among the educated middle-classes of Europe and America.

In Ireland such awareness was articulated in 'The Scandinavian Report' which, besides asserting a need to give greater recognition to hand knits and tweeds in the economy, also highlighted the value of small craft workshops as an adjunct to industry. It pointed to the contribution of small enterprise in acting as a stimulus to industry and the capacity of smaller producers to serve as innovators for new design concepts and developments.[10] The argument underlies much of the designer-craft movement 'that the craftsperson offered a pre-industrial legitimacy that would indirectly ennoble the eventual mass-produced object.'[11] A letter in the Cleo archive reflects this awareness and equally a growing unease over the disappearance of craft skills. Writing in 1959, the venerable design and furniture firm Heal's of London explained their decision to hold 'an exhibition of the work of craftsmen working in the British Isles'. Because 'we find in our travels abroad, that propaganda for the British Craftsman hardly exists. We hope to attract attention to the fact that he does exist.... [so that] much more could be done for his prestige'. (A similar exhibition at Heal's had inspired Muriel Gahan on a visit to London in 1933).[12]

When invited to show in Heal's 1960 exhibition, in Tottenham Court Road, Cleo sent a selection of knits, three of which were chosen and all sold.

Thus, while overseas appreciation sustained Cleo's aim of supporting individual crafts people and maintaining a stock of quality work, they continued to receive little support from middle-class Irish buyers or from Irish government agencies promoting fashion, tourism or the crafts. Just one solitary letter in the archive hints at any custom being directed towards Cleo, indicating how, at least then, they were viewed from an official perspective. Nothing of the style and romance of Cleo's clothes is suggested. Instead, their reputation for weatherproof warmth is construed merely as utility and practicality:

Hamlay Holdings, Montreal, Quebec. *27.10.75*

Dear Sirs,

Your name was given us by the Irish Export Board... We are looking for heavy Irish fisherman's sweaters, hand knitted of sheep wool in a water repellent quality. It is for the use of men working on the ocean.'

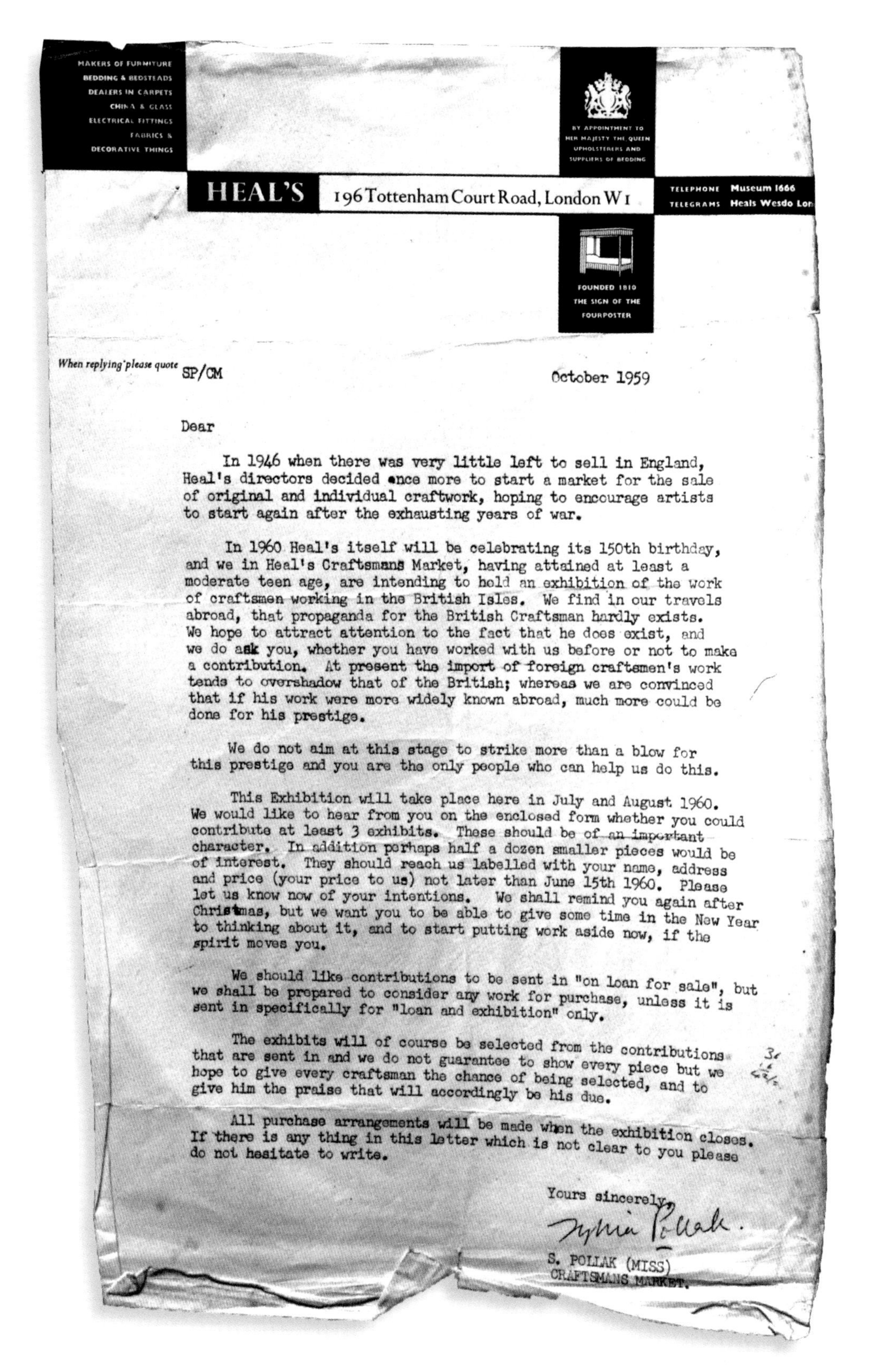

MAKERS OF FURNITURE
BEDDING & BEDSTEADS
DEALERS IN CARPETS
CHINA & GLASS
ELECTRICAL FITTINGS
FABRICS &
DECORATIVE THINGS

BY APPOINTMENT TO HER MAJESTY THE QUEEN UPHOLSTERERS AND SUPPLIERS OF BEDDING

HEAL'S 196 Tottenham Court Road, London W1

TELEPHONE Museum 1666
TELEGRAMS Heals Wesdo Lon

FOUNDED 1810
THE SIGN OF THE FOURPOSTER

When replying please quote SP/CM

October 1959

Dear

In 1946 when there was very little left to sell in England, Heal's directors decided once more to start a market for the sale of original and individual craftwork, hoping to encourage artists to start again after the exhausting years of war.

In 1960 Heal's itself will be celebrating its 150th birthday, and we in Heal's Craftsmans Market, having attained at least a moderate teen age, are intending to hold an exhibition of the work of craftsmen working in the British Isles. We find in our travels abroad, that propaganda for the British Craftsman hardly exists. We hope to attract attention to the fact that he does exist, and we do ask you, whether you have worked with us before or not to make a contribution. At present the import of foreign craftsmen's work tends to overshadow that of the British; whereas we are convinced that if his work were more widely known abroad, much more could be done for his prestige.

We do not aim at this stage to strike more than a blow for this prestige and you are the only people who can help us do this.

This Exhibition will take place here in July and August 1960. We would like to hear from you on the enclosed form whether you could contribute at least 3 exhibits. These should be of an important character. In addition perhaps half a dozen smaller pieces would be of interest. They should reach us labelled with your name, address and price (your price to us) not later than June 15th 1960. Please let us know now of your intentions. We shall remind you again after Christmas, but we want you to be able to give some time in the New Year to thinking about it, and to start putting work aside now, if the spirit moves you.

We should like contributions to be sent in "on loan for sale", but we shall be prepared to consider any work for purchase, unless it is sent in specifically for "loan and exhibition" only.

The exhibits will of course be selected from the contributions that are sent in and we do not guarantee to show every piece but we hope to give every craftsman the chance of being selected, and to give him the praise that will accordingly be his due.

All purchase arrangements will be made when the exhibition closes. If there is any thing in this letter which is not clear to you please do not hesitate to write.

Yours sincerely,

Sylvia Pollak.

S. POLLAK (MISS)
CRAFTSMANS MARKET.

Pinned into a Cleo order book is this letter discussing the demise of craft skills. It is one of several from Heal's, in London.

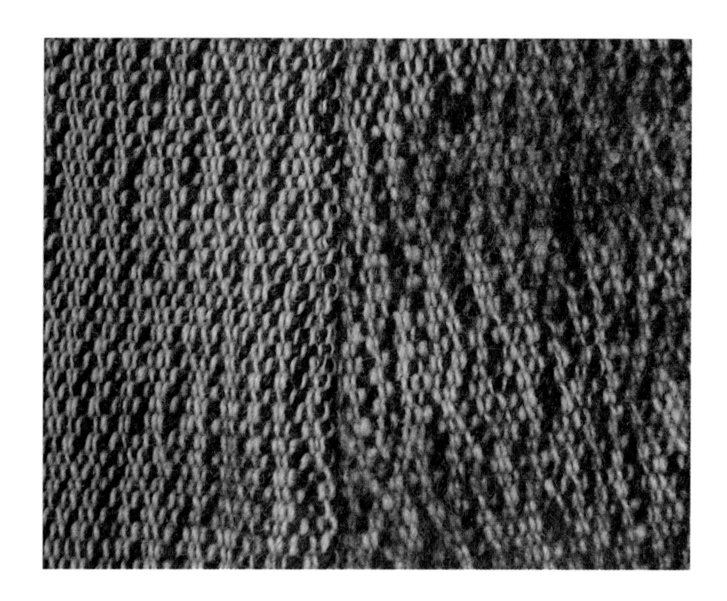

Detail of the Aran homespun tweed featured in the Edward McGuire portrait of Garech Browne. Both sitter and painter were sensitive to its very special weave, almost like flowing water. (Courtesy the Hon. Garech Browne)

HERITAGE

When it comes to the promotion of Irish heritage government policy seems to have concentrated firmly on the language, history and archaeology of Ireland. Other 'living' aspects of Irish culture were long passed over, for example, vernacular architecture, music and clothing. However, one prominent champion of Irish music also shared, and became an important promoter of, Cleo's vision of Irish clothing.

Like leading supporters of the architectural heritage movement, The Irish Georgian Society, Garech Browne comes from a landed, titled background – son of Lady Oranmore and Browne, the early supporter of Cleo. Indeed Garech and his brother Tara had already worn clothes from The Aran Islands and from Cleo since childhood.

Garech Browne's innovative record label Claddagh Records (founded 1959) aimed at and achieved the promoting of Irish traditional music. He regarded the widespread dismissal of local or native culture by people who were not themselves participants as an unfortunate snobbery based on Victorian middle-class notions of Irishness. He mentions, for example, an occasion on which he asked the poet Patrick Kavanagh if he liked Irish music, and Kavanagh replied that he hated it. But when musicians came in to play, Kavanagh's toes started tapping and Browne thought – 'No you don't hate it – you love it – it's part of who you are'.[13] Browne was not alone in thinking that to admit to liking traditional music was to be regarded as completely outdated – nobody aspiring to be Irish and 'modern' would admit a taste for what was often referred to as 'didley-i-tunes'. The wider aim of Claddagh records became, then, to represent traditional music in a new context, to help revive a proud heritage and establish a more positive relationship with tradition for younger Irish musicians.

In 1968 Garech Browne was painted by the great Edward McGuire, painter of many illustrious literary figures including Seamus Heaney, Patrick Kavanagh and Francis Stuart. Neither artist nor sitter were strangers to fashionable society. The artist was a McGuire of Brown Thomas (Dublin's most prestigious department store) and the sitter, the son of an aristocratic and glamorous couple and himself part of 'swinging' London and Dublin society. The image in the portrait however is not one of fashion, but a rather more complex dialogue with dress. Browne is dressed head-to-toe in Irish clothing, of the kind sold in Cleo. By 1968 however such attire was seen less and less even in rural Ireland. He wears an Aran sweater with Aran homespun trousers, which in Browne's case were made by his own tailor, as were all his tweeds. He also wears hand knit stockings and around his waist, a crios. The whole outfit is grounded with stout brown leather shoes.

Garech Browne, painted by Edward McGuire, 1968. Browne's clothing and attributes declare both his support of traditional culture and his lineage from one of the fourteen tribes of Galway. At the same time, they place him at the vanguard of a newly fashionable appreciation for pre-industrial dress, music and culture. Courtesy The Hon. Dr. Garech Browne. Photo by Denis Mortell.

The traditional footwear of the Aran Islands, pampooties, would have made a 'costume' of the outfit because the cowhide slippers had no place outside the Western seaboard where they could be worn in and out of the sea, but these other elements of dress had some place in a wider world. An Aran sweater, particularly, had a traditional music association since Claddagh Records' first recording featured a picture of piper Liam Rowesome in an Aran sweater and the Clancy brothers famously wore them on America's Ed Sullivan Show in 1961. Garech Browne's clothing could be seen to reinforce his musical ambitions of valuing an Irish culture disregarded by the establishment.

The Aran sweater Browne wears is particularly special, not the run-of-the-mill product Carol Brown refers to in a letter to Cleo of the same year as the portrait:

> ... I still wish more of them came with a different set of stitches, much as I admire the usual...which I call SHANNON because so many people come here with Shannon-bought ones in those stitches, and I like to have something different.

In the same letter she wonders 'what the knitters are going to do:

> won't the Aran sweater bubble burst... that sounds like a lot of money on advertising... when they get too common people stop buying' (Dec 23 1968)

Garech Browne is dressed in a way most middle-class people would not dream of risking in the 1960s – or ever really. In a modernising Ireland associations with 'traditional' dress could provoke ridicule. The most prevalent image of west of Ireland dress was in the painting of Seán Keating (1889-1977), who, as an artist, had become perceived as an icon of conservatism. Even in the Dáil, (Ireland's legislative assembly) dress of the west of Ireland has often been a byword for backwardness. In the 1930s James Dillon hectored the Government over their economic policies, saying that even they would see the failure of a 'self sufficient' Ireland when they found the country barefoot and themselves forced to attend The Dáil in báinín.[14] Fifty years later, when Senator Pól 'Báinín' Ó Foighil wore an Aran jacket into the Seanad, he was censured for improper dress. Similarly Garech Browne was refused entry to the Shelbourne Hotel when dressed in his báiníns, and to the Ritz Hotel in London. He was only admitted to Ireland's premier hotel by insisting he was wearing the national dress – his argument later bolstered with a solicitor's letter.[15]

THE WORLD CRAFTS COUNCIL

The attitude Garech Browne describes, of Irish people wishing to put a clear distance between themselves and traditional music, is one even more acutely felt in relation to dress, dress being more visibly related to personal identity than music. Wearing a work of craft can appear a 'badge' proclaiming allegiance to a particular credo.[16] A lack of recognition locally is one reason Cleo were surprised and overwhelmed by the tremendous attention they received in Dublin in the summer of 1970, when the city was honoured as the venue for the fourth World Crafts Council.

This international craft gathering was organised at the Royal Dublin Society (RDS) Ballsbridge, and accompanied by two exhibitions, one in the host venue, and the other in Trinity College. The RDS exhibition presented international craft while the New Library in Trinity showed Irish craftwork, including a Cleo sweater knit in natural grey wools with an oily texture. It is characteristic that Kitty recalls the cooperative aspect of the event, rather than the competitive. She describes 'lending' a sweater to this exhibition, whereas newspaper accounts report a selected show with a '1,000 entries submitted and only 100 pieces selected by an international jury, including Benno Premsela of Holland.'[17]

What Kitty dwells on today is not the assessment of the judges but the appreciative response of this international craft community to the work. Representing Cleo in Trinity was 'one very intricate good dark sweater' – and suddenly, she says, 'people were queuing up'. She describes vividly the shop in Molesworth Street filled with people, even queues out the door and up the steps, with sweaters and cash being exchanged over people's heads. The quality of handmade goods available in Cleo clearly contrasted with what was then more commonly for sale, and the visiting craftspeople were keen to take home from Ireland both a souvenir of their visit but also a useful and practical example of the sort of traditional craft skill they were here to foster. Cleo felt a great wave of appreciation for their work and values. Such acclaim from people they respected gave the shop great encouragement.

COUNTERING 'THE TROUBLES'

This boost would prove vital and sustaining for the shop through the next period of economic, political and industrial difficulties both in Ireland and abroad. When in February 1971 the first soldier, Gunner Robert Curtis, was killed in Northern Ireland, Kitty realised immediately her custom with Britain was doomed. And indeed her order book, built up patiently over the previous decades, did fade away along with visitors from Britain. As well as being a human tragedy in the North, the sectarian Troubles proved a huge impediment to trade. This was soon compounded by oil crises, galloping inflation and widespread industrial disputes. As the mainstay of their business, British custom and the wider tourist trade, rapidly died away Cleo considered where and how to develop new markets, and in January 1972 placed an advertisement in *The New Yorker* magazine.

The small, plain black and white picture features a fine Aran polo neck sweater with a complicated stitch, laid on a hard peg board surface. The copy reads:

> *Traditional Aran pullover in natural white.*
> *There are no two patterns alike.*
> *Comes also with crew neck.*
> *Women's sizes - 36" thru 40"*
> *Cost Overseas $29.09 Air $ 34.00*
> *Men's sizes - 38" thru 48" - Give Height*
> *Cost Overseas $32.45 Air $37.80*
> *Personal cheques acceptable.*
> *We have been mailing to U.S. since 1945.*
> *Send $1 for colour brochure of our couture and sports*
> *handknit and handwoven goods with yarn samples*
> *enclosed*

The cost of advertising in *The New Yorker* meant Cleo opted for less than a quarter page space, and certainly no colour, but the impact on sales merited retaining the advertisement over two years. Though the image featured a much less stylish picture than had appeared in Ireland's *Creation* magazine almost twenty years earlier, it proved worth repeating and updating in many later issues. The

A Cleo advertisement in *The New Yorker* magazine, January 15 1972. An American reading of Aran knitting was highlighted when customers ordering sweaters by post, referring to the three-dimensional 'bobailín' or blackberry stitch, would request more or less 'popcorn' on their sweaters.

order book contains many clippings of the ad cut from the magazine to accompany orders. Cleo also experimented with an advertisement for a fringed shawl. Only one of these survives, tucked into the order book, and it does look rather doleful - the only person to order it, Kitty remembers, mentioned they had been motivated by pity.

In 1973, with the oil crisis deepening and tourist numbers plummeting further, Cleo sought to improve their American sales with a revised *New Yorker* advertisement. A new photo, featuring the sweaters being worn by friends and relatives of the shop, is accompanied by the message:

Keep warm during The Crisis in Organic Handknits from Ireland. 100% natural unbleached wool; oils left in for weather repellency. Pullover (specify crew or turtleneck).

Ladies' 36 - 40: Sea $33; Air $38 Men's 42-48: Sea $36; Air $42

Matching hats...

Whether helped by the oil crisis or the updated image is not clear, but sales increased and the advertisement was repeated in several versions over the next two years. Cleo may have benefitted from discussing advertising strategy with their long-time American customer and friend Janet Livingstone, who was by this time running the Kilkenny Design franchise in San Francisco.

Janet advised Cleo on pricing, quality and advertising copy, forwarding examples of comparable magazine ads appearing in the USA:

...I would price the sweater, below $40.00 if possible....then I would ask them to add $5.00 for air post .. or whatever the general rate is. This makes the sweater price look less...But there must be some good copy about the knitters and the price of wool and your insistence on quality and individuality of sweaters...[and giving knitters a raise]. I would charge a really good price and send out only sweaters of the quality that I pick when I am there – really be careful on mail orders. Save the dogs for bargaining when someone is in the shop.

(Letter 15.12.72)

This Cleo advertisement, also placed in *The New Yorker,* highlights (by their absence) the value of specialist skills in presenting knitwear on a flat page.

One ad Janet sent for comparative purposes was from a shop in Princeton, its jumper featuring that rather uninventive pattern of diamonds and what the American customers called 'waffle' pattern, a stitch known in Ireland as 'honeycomb'. Despite its lack of originality the place in Princeton was asking more ($48) than Cleo did ($40–$45) for something much more individual sent from further afield.

Cleo's 'Janet Jacket', named after Janet Livingstone, a customer and friend, has been in production since the 1970s and is still selling, to both men and women.

PROMOTION

The knitwear images Cleo first used in *The New Yorker* were taken from a promotional sheet they relied on, since about 1964, to illustrate their price list and act as advertising and promotion.

In the later 1960s those informative if somewhat rigid photographs were replaced with more lively and fashionable interpretations of the clothes drawn up by Denise Morris, a new, young addition to Cleo's staff at the time.

Denise's felt-tip marker drawings, capturing a more youthful feeling in the Cleo stock, were xeroxed and sent to retailers abroad to help them place orders. They appear to have been greatly appreciated, as Carol Brown asks for 25–30 of the sketches 'if they are available'. Occasionally they are cut up and appear in the order books sent by a distant customer to identify the particular garment they wanted. It may have been the success of the Denise drawings that prompted Kitty to look for something further 'to explain the clothes a bit better' and in 1970 she contacted Bill Doyle, now known as 'Ireland's Cartier-Bresson' who had only recently set up as a freelance photographer.

Example No. 3 and 4 price list.

Comes also without buttoning to collar tip and in round neck.

Cleo

3 Molesworth Street

(opposite Hibernian Hotel)

Dublin

Ireland

Phone
73408

Example No. 1 and 2 price list.

Comes also in crew neckline.

IN OUR STORE you will find a variety of marvellous hand-knit sweaters, made for generations by the cottage folk of the West of Ireland in their own traditional designs. The wool used is scoured unbleached, and ranges in tone from cream to oatmeal. The sheep's oil remaining in the wool lends a water repellant character to the sweater. The wool is of extraordinary toughness—long wearing—non-shrinking. Each knitter presents a different pattern all of remarkable intricacy. Sweaters such as these are admirable for any outdoor activity or just to keep warm.

Children's sweaters come as miniatures of the adult ones.

In the same family are caps, mitts and gloves.

Our hand-knit shawls in self colours and multicolours fringed all around are ideal for evening wear.

In the hand-woven section come hand-woven peasant belts called crios, woven traditionally in six colours. They encircle the waist twice, leaving tasselled ends hanging. In the same group and derived from the crios is the crios hat and scarf.

Avoca hand-woven rugs come in brilliant and perfectly blended colours to brighten the picnic, lend warmth to the car and gaiety to a dull room.

Example No. 19 price list.

The black and white promotional sheet used by Cleo throughout much of the 1960s.
Addressing an international audience, it describes itself as a store, a term not yet widely used in Ireland, for a shop.

The Cleo range, hand drawn by Denise Morris who worked in Cleo, xeroxed for distribution to customers abroad.

Kitty had known Bill Doyle for years through hill walking and he had taken their wedding photos when she and Tom Joyce married in 1961. Tom is originally from Co. Mayo but moved to Co. Dublin where he and Kitty went on to have six children, while he ran a farm in the mountains and she ran the business in town. This would not have been possible without their mutual support and the help of a committed work force. Kitty always acknowledges the support Tom gives to Cleo in myriad ways, including looking after the six children while also farming. It is interesting to note that while Kitty and Tom Joyce had a family of six children during the 1960s and '70s they did not apply for any children's allowance. Just as Kit Ryan had decided, in the 1930s and '40s, she could sustain herself, her family and her business without leaning on the new government for the widow's pension, so her daughter and son-in-law chose to survive without the government subsidy, that is until tax laws in Ireland changed and they 'considered the Government were overburdening the business people'.

In about 1970 Kitty asked Bill Doyle to take some colour shots of Cleo clothes in settings around Dublin. She selected the garments and he picked the locations. Tom Joyce brought bales of hay from the farm and models were chosen from among friends and relations, women working in the shop and the Joyce children. On the Saint Patrick's Day bank holiday, this troupe headed down the Liffey to a quiet cul-de-sac by the docks and the result was a series of simple, charming photos of Irish hand knitting, tweeds and wools.

The promotional shoot then moved to the Sally Gap in Wicklow where a knitted poncho, trousers and cap were modelled alongside one of Tom Joyce's ponies draped in a 'spectrum' rug.

An urban, and perhaps 'Georgian', contrast to the rural scenes was created with a photograph of two women in richly coloured Kinsale cloaks on the steps of the Mansion House, in Dawson Street. The elegance of this, the Lord Mayor's house, Kitty notes was helped by Bill Doyle sweeping away all the cigarette butts left from the St Patrick's Day parade.

The new colour brochure for the first time caught how colourful Cleo clothes were and suggested the sort of world they came from. Again it was greatly appreciated by customers overseas:

'Dear Kitty,

Thank you so much for your recent brochure of lovely, beautiful, fantastic, marvellous, knitted goods. Could you send as soon as possible the following...

(Claude Baliey, N.Y. USA, 30 October 1970).

While Cleo was negotiating its way through a modernising Ireland, Tom and Kitty Joyce, married since 1961, were rearing a growing family, running a farm in the Dublin mountains and the shop in town. Here they appear with four of their six children, on the occasion of Mark's first Holy Communion, c.1973. From right to left, Mary, Kitty, (wearing linen handprinted by a textile designer working above Cleo in Molesworth Street) Mark, Bryan, Tom, Helen and a school friend of Mary's. The two youngest children (not present) are Stephen and Sarah. The picture was taken in St Stephen's Green by Kitty's friend, photographer Bill Doyle, who had a studio there.

Opposite and following page: Images from Cleo's 1970 colour brochure achieved a further updating of their promotional profile. Compositions conceived of as 'Old Ireland' presented alongside more contemporary looks suggest Cleo were unconcerned or unaware about any rigid fixing of their position. Photographed by Bill Doyle (details) models: friends and relations of Cleo and Bill Doyle.

Also strengthening the sense of their connection with rural Ireland, and as a complement to the brochure, Bill Doyle licensed Cleo to use one of his now famous 1940s photographs as their correspondence card.

AMERICAN IRISH SHOPS

The *New Yorker* advertisements continued to help sales hold up in difficult times, but what really carried Cleo through much of the 1970s was the mushrooming of 'Irish shops' across America. They were, as Carol Brown said:

> 'springing up all over. . .many of them complete with crystal, pottery, lace etc. etc. etc. etc. .. as Irish Imports ... A man from Ottawa is due here tomorrow . . .

Cleo's 1970 colour brochure carried their image for almost a decade, through three changes of address. In this cover image an Aran knit poncho, tousers and 'Tam' are worn alongside Tom Joyce's pony draped in a spectrum rug.

Modelling a Kinsale cloak, on the steps of the Mansion House, Brenda Smyth (facing camera) was the first non-family employee of Cleo. She worked wth Cleo on and off over many years, and as an air hostess with Aer Lingus.

Cleo used, under license from the photographer, this Bill Doyle image to emphasise their connection with traditional life. Printed as a postcard on photographic paper the caption reads:

Thatched Cottage, Clogher Head, Co. Louth
With thick puddled mud walls.
Small windows prevent heat loss. Half door keeps animals out and promotes community living.

contemplating opening an Irish shop there, and is down here inspecting Irish shops.' (27 March 1975)

While some were substantial enterprises, others were run almost as a pastime, mostly by women with an affinity for Ireland, whose families had grown up. 'A Wee Bit O Ireland', 'The Luckpenny Store' and the 'Erin Import Shoppe' give a flavour of different businesses represented by diverse headed papers tucked into Cleo's order books.

Running these small shops allowed women enjoy a connection with 'home' or Ireland while developing relations with their American community. It was also a way of earning a little money. But to make it worth their while owners had to avoid paying import taxes. This was made possible through a loop allowing small value imports into America tax-free. Orders placed by the small shops therefore were sometimes accompanied by a request to:

please ship orders in lots of £100 or less on different days. We have found when checking with customs that when an order exceeds $240 or £100 we must use a customs broker to bring the merchandise into the U.S. This costs an additional 7%. (2 June 1971).

The American import duties resulted in additional work for Cleo but also in more business, and proved satisfactory until trade was interrupted, first by Irish industrial relations and then through tax-law changes under the Reagan administration.

INDUSTRIAL DISPUTES AND SHORTAGES

This burgeoning American export trade was seriously threatened by the four-month postal strike in Ireland in 1979. Instead of the short trip to South Anne Street Post Office, Cleo had to package their orders in corrugated cardboard as well as the usual brown paper and twine, fill the car with parcels and drive to the North of Ireland, to avail of the British postal service. Shipping the orders was not the only hurdle, however, as the postal strike coincided with the second severe petrol shortage of the decade. If Kitty ran low on petrol halfway through the journey she could have real difficulty getting a local garage owner to sell any of a precious supply to a passing driver. Most garages tried to keep their petrol for local customers. So Kitty would have to park by the petrol station until a regular was served and then drive in immediately to dissuade the owner from claiming they were empty. When she did reach the North she had to contend with the risk of her Royal Mail shipments being destroyed by security services if it was discovered that these suspect looking brown parcels in fact originated in the Republic. While all these problems were time consuming and awkward, solutions could at least be found using imagination and energy. Both were commodities

215-862-9285

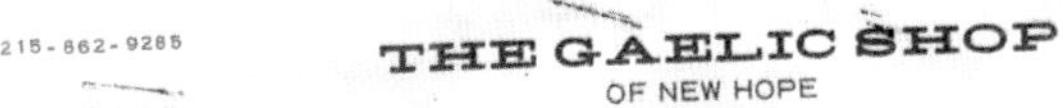

THE GAELIC SHOP
OF NEW HOPE
~~76 SOUTH MAIN STREET~~ P.O. Box 6
NEW HOPE, PENNSYLVANIA 18938 USA

29 December 1976

Cleo, Limited
35 Dawson Street
Dublin
Ireland

MOLLY'S BARROW
GAELIC IMPORTS, LTD.
ALL FROM IRELAND
1492 OLD KING'S HIGHWAY
WEST BARNSTABLE, MASS. 02668

617-834-6252

MRS. P. D. McCORMACK
~~BOX 305~~
~~GREEN HARBOR, MASS.~~

TEL. 846

THE IRISH DANDELION
IRISH HANDKNITS
CRAFTS

BRICK MARKET PLACE NEWPORT, R. I.

Complete as possible – needs 2 Aran

Feb. 28,1977

Hello,
It is alovely sunny day here as I write and we are beginning to believe that spring may be coming.

I like to order the following:
6 waistcoats -mens size 38,40(2)
42(2)
44(1)

Substituting Womens aran patterns for women # 33

6 " Womens size 32(2
34(2

Feeney and daughters
DESIGNS FROM IRELAND

February 22, 1977

Mrs. K. Ryan
Cleo Ltd.
35 Dawson Street
Dublin

Dear Mrs. Ryan:

(314) 726-1188

shannon shop
Irish Handcrafts

Tom Littmann

8215 Clayton Road
Clayton, Missouri 63105

A selection of business cards and letterheads from Cleo's order books are testament to the burgeoning of Irish American shops all over the United States.

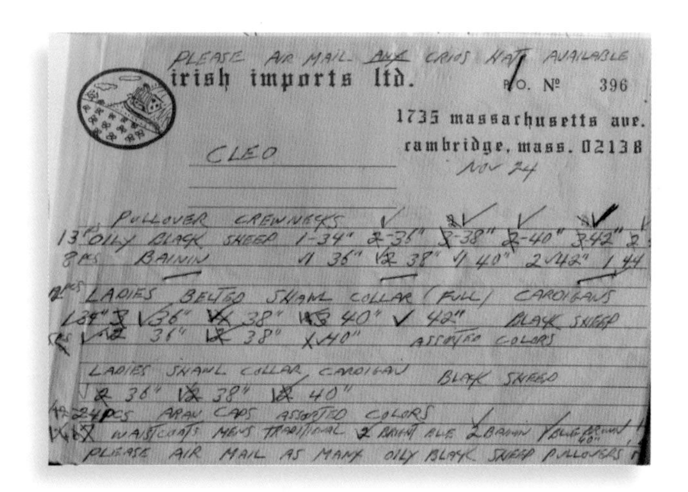

PLEASE AIR MAIL ANY CRIOS HATS AVAILABLE

irish imports ltd. P.O. № 396

1735 massachusetts ave.
cambridge, mass. 02138

CLEO

NOV 24

PULLOVER CREWNECKS

13 OILY BLACK SHEEP 1-34" 2-36" 3-38" 2-40" 3-42"

8 PCS BAININ 1 36" 2 38" 1 40" 2 42" 1 44

LADIES BELTED SHAWL COLLAR (FULL) CARDIGANS

34" 36" 38" 40" 42" BLACK SHEEP

36" 38" 40" ASSORTED COLORS

LADIES SHAWL COLLAR CARDIGAN BLACK SHEEP

36" 38" 40"

24 PCS ARAN CAPS ASSORTED COLORS

WAISTCOATS MENS TRADITIONAL 2 BRIGHT BLUE 2 BAININ 1 BLUE BROWN 40"

PLEASE AIR MAIL AS MANY OILY BLACK SHEEP PULLOVERS

'Irish Imports', run by Mike and Virginia Shiels in Cambridge, Massachusetts since 1973, remains one of Cleo's best American customers.

Kitty remembers Cleo having in abundance in the 1970s with a bright, energetic team including many members of the now famous musical Black family. The younger set was complemented by the more experienced Brenda Smyth, and Kitty's contemporaries Mrs Marie Murtagh and Mrs Hanne Burke who, with meticulous care, looked after big numbers of small orders. Marie Murtagh, the school friend of Kitty's who came to Cleo in the early 1970s, having raised a family, brought 'the great energy of someone leaving the pinning down of home.' Hanne Burke, a neighbour of Marie's, was a German woman married to an Irishman, and also mother of a family. 'She was a wonderful person' says Kitty who clearly relished the skills and company of these women. 'In the 1970s there was so much retail business happening as well as export business and we had the people to do it.'

While energy and application alleviated many difficulties, they could make little impact on the galloping inflation that left 'businesses and customers punch drunk'. The Cleo price list that had barely changed through the 1950s and '60s had to be adjusted and reprinted several times in a single year. For twenty years or more, until the early 1970s, the price of a lady's Aran sweater or 'coat sweater', as the Americans sometimes called cardigans, had remained about £4.10.0. But by 1976 it cost £13.50 in 'new money'. By January 1977 it was £15.00 and by April the same year it had risen to £16.50. The sudden increases drew some aghast queries from overseas customers:

> *'Orders have cost much more than I had expected from your original price list. I do hope that I will not have to pay … on the basis of your new price list since they were ordered prior to January 1972 and I based my prices on the former list'* (13 December 1971)

Inflation was one problem, but another was customers' dismay at finding it might not be possible to have their order completed following a rapid decline in the number of knitters available. One letter from Georgetown (July 19th 1977) reads:

> *'You mentioned in your letter you could ship next February. Are you serious, because we would then totally miss the Christmas business, not to speak of this Fall'.*

And a letter from Nantucket (January 1977) suggests the sorts of rearrangements necessitated by this sudden decline:

> *Dear Mrs Ryan,*
>
> *We laboured and laboured over which sweaters were most important according to requests and popularity. (We have added a second order, which we hope you will do your best to fill in time.) I am afraid we have become*

known throughout for the Cleo Aran knit sweater. We have requests daily for it and could easily sell triple the amount. (Upstairs, Downstairs Ltd)

No period seemed more of a struggle than the 1970s, that is until the recent worldwide economic downturn. But of all the difficulties that were to follow during the 1970s the hardest of all for Kitty was the enforced move of her business from Molesworth Street. In 1950 Mrs Ryan had taken on the basement of No. 3 a 21-year lease she felt "would see her out". She was not mistaken, and she did remain into her 70s at the helm of the city-centre, international business she had established and built. When she died aged 75 (8 Jan. 1964) her passing elicited little to suggest the contribution her consummate work had made to sustain Ireland's reputation for quality wool and linen through the 20th century. With

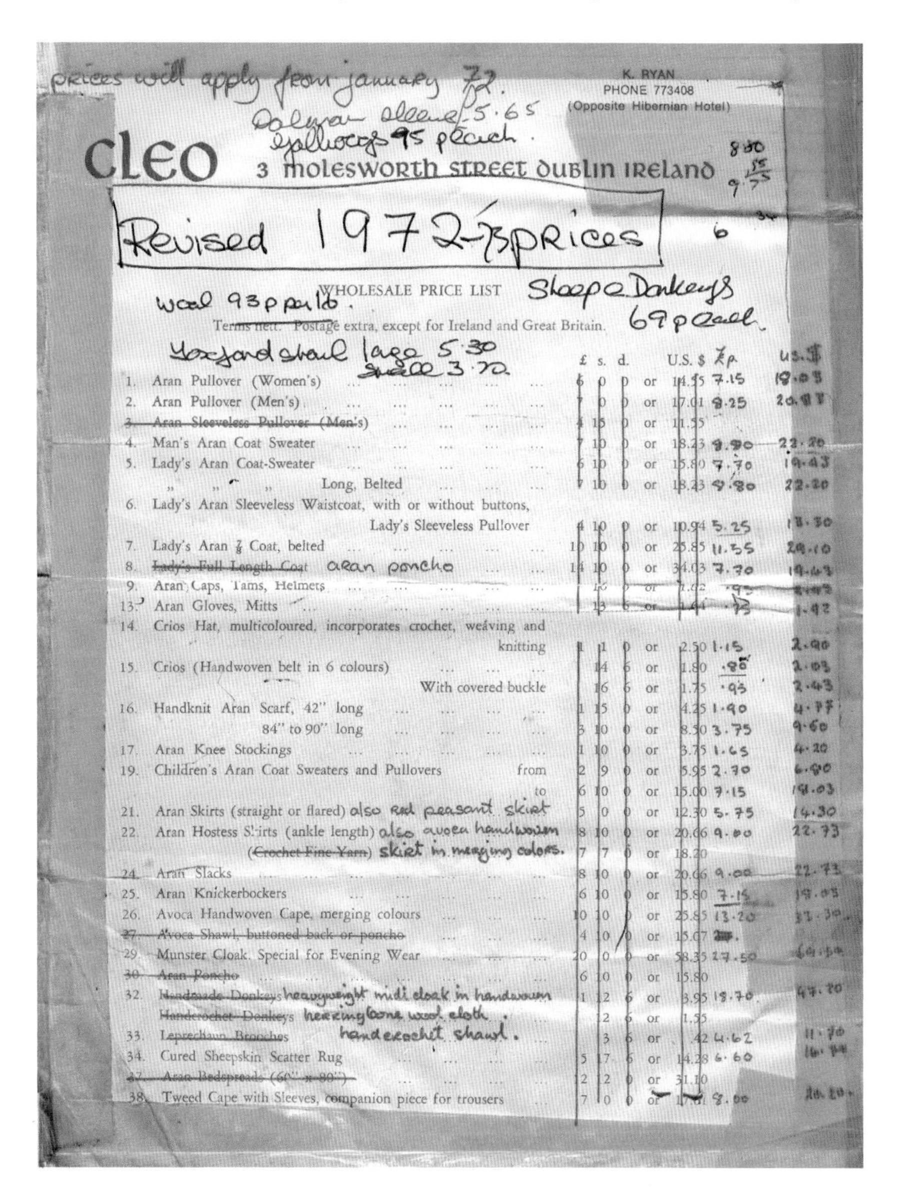

prices will apply from january 72.

K. RYAN
PHONE 773408
(Opposite Hibernian Hotel)

CLEO 3 MOLESWORTH STREET DUBLIN IRELAND

Revised 1972-73 PRICES

WHOLESALE PRICE LIST

wool 93p per lb.

Sheep & Donkeys 69p each.

~~Terms nett.~~ Postage extra, except for Ireland and Great Britain.

No.	Item	£	s.	d.		U.S. $	£p	U.S. $
1.	Aran Pullover (Women's)	6	0	0	or	14.55	7.15	18.03
2.	Aran Pullover (Men's)	7	0	0	or	17.01	8.25	20.87
~~3.~~	~~Aran Sleeveless Pullover (Men's)~~	4	15	0	or	11.55		
4.	Man's Aran Coat Sweater	7	10	0	or	18.23	8.90	22.20
5.	Lady's Aran Coat-Sweater	6	10	0	or	15.80	7.70	19.43
	" " " Long, Belted	7	10	0	or	18.23	8.80	22.20
6.	Lady's Aran Sleeveless Waistcoat, with or without buttons, Lady's Sleeveless Pullover	4	10	0	or	10.94	5.25	13.30
7.	Lady's Aran ⅞ Coat, belted	10	10	0	or	25.85	11.55	29.10
8.	~~Lady's Full Length Coat~~ aran poncho	14	10	0	or	34.03	7.70	19.43
9.	Aran Caps, Tams, Helmets (crossed out in pen)		16	0	or	[illegible]	.95	[illegible]
13.	Aran Gloves, Mitts (crossed out in pen)		13	6	or	[illegible]	[illegible]	1.42
14.	Crios Hat, multicoloured, incorporates crochet, weaving and knitting	1	1	0	or	2.50	1.15	2.90
15.	Crios (Handwoven belt in 6 colours)		14	6	or	1.80	.80	2.03
	With covered buckle		16	6	or	1.75	.95	2.43
16.	Handknit Aran Scarf, 42" long	1	15	0	or	4.25	1.90	4.77
	84" to 90" long	3	10	0	or	8.50	3.75	9.60
17.	Aran Knee Stockings	1	10	0	or	3.75	1.65	4.20
19.	Children's Aran Coat Sweaters and Pullovers from	2	9	0	or	5.95	2.70	6.80
	to	6	10	0	or	15.00	7.15	18.03
21.	Aran Skirts (straight or flared) also red peasant skirt	5	0	0	or	12.30	5.75	14.30
22.	Aran Hostess Skirts (ankle length) also avoca handwoven	8	10	0	or	20.66	9.00	22.73
	(~~Crochet Fine Yarn~~) skirt in merging colors.	7	7	6	or	18.20		
~~24.~~	~~Aran Slacks~~	8	10	0	or	20.66	9.00	22.73
25.	Aran Knickerbockers	6	10	0	or	15.80	7.15	18.03
26.	Avoca Handwoven Cape, merging colours	10	10	0	or	25.85	13.20	33.30
~~27.~~	~~Avoca Shawl, buttoned back or poncho~~	4	10	0	or	15.07	[illegible]	
29.	Munster Cloak. Special for Evening Wear	20	0	0	or	58.35	27.50	69.50
~~30.~~	~~Aran Poncho~~	6	10	0	or	15.80		
32.	~~Handmade Donkeys~~ heavyweight midi cloak in handwoven	1	12	6	or	3.95	18.70	47.20
	~~Handcrochet Donkeys~~ herringbone wool cloth.		2	6	or	1.55		
33.	~~Leprechaun Brooches~~ handcrochet shawl.		3	6	or	.42	4.62	11.70
34.	Cured Sheepskin Scatter Rug	5	17	6	or	14.28	6.60	[illegible]
~~37.~~	~~Aran Bedspreads (60" x 80")~~	12	12	0	or	31.10		
38.	Tweed Cape with Sleeves, companion piece for trousers	7	0	0	or	[illegible]	8.00	20.20

Cleo price list 1971-2, with adjustments for inflation. After decades of stability, inflation in the 1970s saw rises so rapid that even re-printing price lists several times in one year could not keep pace with increases.

slight reflection of her achievement as a craftswoman and entrepreneur, her death certificate records her occupation as simply 'shopkeeper'.

Molesworth Street had proven a wonderful location for Cleo, but when the lease expired it could not be renewed. Despite the outrage of conservationists, much of the Georgian and Victorian streetscape of Molesworth Street was razed, making way for modern office blocks. The Georgian house Cleo occupied was scheduled for demolition and they had to move. After much searching Cleo relocated, taking a lease on the basement of 35 Dawson Street, opposite the Mansion House. But Kitty says it never suited them and she never settled in. The only surviving references to this upheaval in the archive (much paperwork having been discarded in the move) are brief mentions in letters from Carol Brown asking 'How is business in the new place?' and hoping 'that pretty soon, you will be enthusiastic about the new shop.' But they never did become enthusiastic and Kitty feels that as soon as she could, in the mid-1970s, 'she just walked out and closed the door...'

Endnotes

1 McCrum, Elizabeth (1996) *Fabric & Form, Irish Fashion Since* 1950, Belfast, Ulster Museum, p. 34.

2 Kilkenny Design Workshops were founded in 1963 with the studio workshops actually opening in 1965. Turpin, John (1986) 'The Irish Design Reform Movement of the 1960s' in *Design Issues*, Vol III.

3 de la Haye, Amy and V. Mendes (1999) *Twentieth Century Fashion*, London, Thames & Hudson. p.165.

4 McCutcheon, Mary (8 December 1971) 'Courreges chooses Ireland for men's clothes'. *Irish Independent*, Independent Woman, p. 11.

5 The report is officially titled *Design in Ireland*. Published 1962 in Dublin. See Caffrey, Paul (1998) 'The Scandinavian Ideal: a model for design in Ireland', *Scandinavian Journal of Design History* 8, pp. 32-43.

6 Córas Tráchtála (1962) *Design in Ireland*, p. 10.

7 Ibid p. 8.

8 O'Kelly, Hilary, in conversation with Michael Molloy in The National Museum Collins Barracks, at the opening of the Néillí Mulcahy exhibition. (October 17 2007)

9 For a similar account see also Sayers Nuttall, Meghan (2001) 'Conversations in Donegal: Mary McNeillis and Con O'Gara' *New Hibernia Review* 5.3, p.16.

See also documentary on 'The Weaver's Shed' in David Shaw Smith's *Hands* Series, No. 6, available www.irelandstraditionalcrafts.com.

10 Córas Tráchtála (1962) *Design In Ireland* p. 21.

11 Adamson, Glenn (2007) *Thinking Through Craft*, Oxford, New York, Berg, p.105.

12 Mitchell, Geraldine (1997) *Deeds Not Words: The Life and Work of Muriel Gahan*, Dublin,Town House, p.108.

13 Cranitch, Evelyn (8 March 2010) Interview with Garech Browne, Raidió Teilifís Éireann (RTÉ) Lyric FM.

14 Dáil Éireann (12 May 1933) debates.oireachtas.ie/dail/1933/05/12, [978]

15 O'Kelly, Hilary (13 October 2011) in conversation with Garech Browne, Luggala, Co Wicklow.

16 Adamson, Glenn (2007) *Thinking Through Craft*, Oxford, New York, Berg, p. 21.

17 'Irish Craftwork on Exhibition; 100 Items selected' (12 August 1970) *The Irish Times*, p. 8.

Opposite: 'Fisherman's Trousers' added to the Cleo range in the 1970s, modelled by Diarmuid Boyd, son-in-law of Kitty Joyce, and painter of the image of the shop on Cleo correspondence cards. Model Corina Grant wears a crios hat, Aran knit sweater and also 'Fisherman's Trousers'.

KILDARE STREET

The Fabric of the Nation

A NEW LOCATION

The political turmoil and architectural demolition in Dublin during the mid-1970s coincided with a deep recession. As unemployment and emigration persisted, both retail and property markets remained stagnant. A Georgian house in Kildare Street had languished on the market for several years before being spotted by Tom Joyce, who was aware of Kitty's dissatisfaction with the shop in Dawson Street. He suggested it might make a better option for Cleo, and this time not to lease but to buy.

"Cleo's is the best shop in Ireland. It's not big, it doesn't sell a lot of things, and it's not glitzy. All it has is handknit sweaters..."

Number 18 Kildare Street is one of a small number of Georgian houses on a stretch now dominated by important institutions including the seat of Government; the Dáil, the National Museum, and National Library, the Department of Finance, the Department of Agriculture and the Royal College of Physicians. At the northern end, towards St Stephen's Green, this stern official face is humanised by smaller establishments, including the Taylor Galleries, de Veres and Adam's auction houses, and Cleo handknits and handweaves.

18 Kildare Street, home of Cleo since c.1974. (Photo by Alan Betson, courtesy *The Irish Times*).

Suits by Cleo, in fabrics from Crock-of-Gold, Blackrock, Co. Dublin. Modelled by professional models Frances Duff (left) and Sonia Reynolds.

Supplied with the daily papers, this corner of Cleo offers respite to flagging spirits, usually those of men accompanying women shoppers. George Nakashima, one of the fathers of the 20th century American crafts movement, made the chairs. The table is by a younger Japanese craftsman.

While all around businesses continued to struggle, fortunately Cleo's American export market was buoyant, so despite the wider difficulties of trade in 1974 Kitty and Tom Joyce decided to buy the Kildare Street building. Its position, close to The Shelbourne, Dublin's landmark hotel, was a significant factor as proximity to the Hibernian Hotel had been so important to Cleo on Molesworth Street. The purchase price – £45,000 – they had already built up, by saving the tax relief on exports to the Irish shops in America. Every human and financial resource they had went into refurbishing the old building. Besides repairing walls, floors and ceilings Kitty concentrated on devising an interior sympathetic to the display of handmade textiles. She commissioned bespoke shelving from Paul Moore, a creative woodworker in Laois, and for the kitchen bought Irish country chairs from Al O'Dea in Tuam, then exceptional in his regard for Irish vernacular furniture. Her instinct for the handmade object – not only Irish – may be seen in another choice, of chairs by the celebrated Japanese-American craftsman, George Nakashima.

As this was the first premises Cleo actually owned, Kitty wanted 'to make a present to the shop' and commissioned from Anthony Hedgecock, an Englishman recently settled in Gortahork, Co. Donegal, custom made-ironwork for the exterior. Drawing on Celtic interlace and old-Irish uncial script, he designed the Cleo shop signage. He also created a lamp-lit arch over the steps to the basement, reminiscent of Cleo in Molesworth Street, which had become known over twenty years for its basement location and nicely dressed window. Then, just as all this extensive refurbishment was completed dry rot was discovered in the building. Cleo responded as ever, with energy and application, and the support of family and friends coming to the rescue. Though it had not been plain sailing, it was still a great reward, after forty years in business, to be able to lay a solid foundation for the future of the shop. The foresight in securing their own premises was proven during the recent economic boom when a business trading in mostly handmade goods could never have met rents, escalating to phenomenal levels.

TAILORS, DRESSMAKERS AND FASHION DESIGNERS

When Cleo bought 18 Kildare Street, in 1974, (and became a limited company), a significant proportion of what Irish people wore was still made in Ireland, particularly shirts and shoes. The industry however was in decline.[1] Rag trade factories still operated across Dublin city, and South William Street was still lined with wholesalers supplying the draperies of Dublin and rural Ireland. Although government policy aimed to support local manufacture the majority of the textile trade ultimately followed cheaper labour around the globe. As the infrastructure of the clothing trade declined, energies moved increasingly to design and marketing. John Rocha, Michael Mortell and Paul Costelloe all launched their own labels in the late '70s, and by the 1980s had won international reputations – though commercial success was more challenging and to a large extent only cemented later abroad. In the 1980s, to retail the work of young fashion designers graduating from newly established art school fashion courses, the Irish Design Centre opened in St Stephen's Green. Meanwhile many women continued to make dresses and children's wear at home, but as shop-clothes became less expensive and more 'easy-care' this practice also declined. The wider impact on retail was that family-run clothing businesses, which had dressed, and even shaped, Irish towns, slowly gave way to shopping centres and later British and European chain stores.

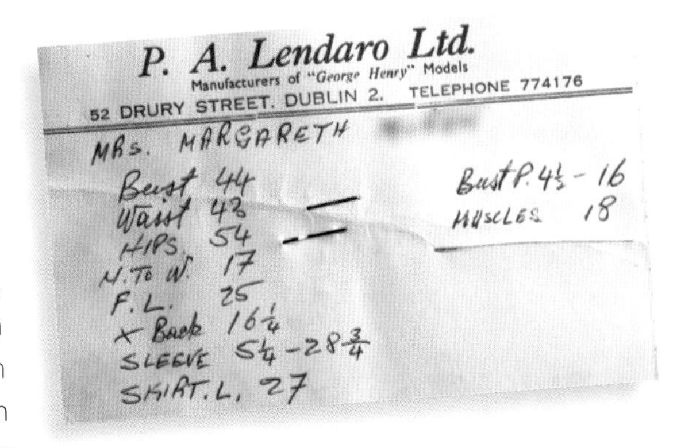

P. A. Lendaro Ltd.
Manufacturers of "George Henry" Models
52 DRURY STREET. DUBLIN 2. TELEPHONE 774176

MRS. MARGARETH
Bust 44
Waist 4⅜
HIPS 54
N. TO W. 17
F.L. 25
x Back 16¼
SLEEVE 5¼-28¾
SKIRT. L. 27

Bust P. 4½ - 16
MUSCLES 18

Tailor Austin Lendaro of Drury Street supplied Cleo, Arnott's of Henry Street, Mc Ilhenny's of Athboy and the cottage industries. (And also, apparently, catered for individual non-standard figure-sizes.)

Tailoring and dressmaking skills had always been essential to Cleo, and since the earliest days they drew on a range of independent tailors and designers who ran their own businesses, selling under their own labels. Later individual makers, recently let go from the manufacturing trade and operating from makeshift premises like a shed in the garden, might supply Cleo with lighter goods – blouses for instance. Government initiatives facilitated some of these operators to expand to industrial estates, employing more people and producing bigger quantities of garments requiring less skill – work uniforms, for example. These manufacturers came to find interrupting the regularity of a production line and initiating a small order for more detailed work unsatisfactory, and it became more difficult for Cleo to find firms willing or able to supply them.

Of the skilled makers once to be found in Dublin City centre, two figures in particular stand out for Cleo. In the 1970s and 1980s they had:

> Austin Lendaro and Vera Hennessy making coats, jackets and skirts in magnificent fabrics. The whole scene floated as these people picked up on what we were doing. It just worked. Austin was a wartime refugee from Italy who spent some time in Glencree, Co. Wicklow. He trained with Jack Clarke of Richard Alan and the people who trained with Jack made excellent tailors. [Richard Alan of Grafton Street has been one of Dublin's best dress shops since opening in 1935]. Austin worked for us for a long time and we had him for his best years. He was a joy. He liked small bulk orders and we were able to give him that. When it came to special orders it was less simple.
>
> One day the person who was the trusted assistant to Mary Robinson came in [to Cleo, in the early 1990s] to order a coat for the President to wear when attending funerals. Austin was so impressed he wanted to order a very special material for the job. I think it was cashmere. I'd remind him to get on with it and he would say "But, Mrs Joyce, she is the President". He would only use the best, and was waiting so long for the material he never got to do it for her.

Austin Lendaro modelling one of the coats he made for Cleo. His skills have been difficult to replace; Kitty says she is 'still giving out to Austin for dying'.

An advertisement for Vera Hennessy featured in *Creation* Magazine, May 1958.

Vera Hennessy also ran her own business as a designer and maker, with a premises in South Anne Street, and a reputation for ball gowns and fashionable sports wear – clothes with an altogether different profile to Cleo's. Vera Hennessy worked for us for years doing the cloaks, suits and other things as well. She was a very good maker with softer, drapier, designs though she was not a tailor'. For Cleo's women's range she made the busman's pocket skirt, culottes, and the Dana Wynter skirt, so named after the svelte actress had purchased one. Kitty describes it as a skirt that 'doesn't accuse you'. It was made in tweed with an elastic waist – which can 'be very frumpy – but Vera had a way with cutting it.'

A notably successful collaboration between Kitty and Vera, christened the 'Creation', was a distinctive garment designed by Kitty based on a top she spotted elsewhere. It had the strange design feature, for an outdoor garment, of a zip running down the back that made it a little awkward for removing elegantly, but it was nonetheless very popular. Stylish, yet stoutly protective in almost waterproof boiled wool from Millars of Clifden, the 'Creation' was a staple of the Cleo range throughout the 1970s:

> When we had Vera and Austin I could see someone in the street wearing something that caught my eye. I could think 'well, that would be good if the front was this or that'. I couldn't draw for my life but I would go over to Austin - or Vera - describe it, and he would draw it. He would produce a sample. He was brilliant. He could do anything for us.
>
> Once there was a woman sitting across from me on a train in Paris. I was with my son Mark and I said, "Draw the front of her coat" Mark had an envelope or something. I put that then with a detail from a coat I had enjoyed at a fair in Germany. Someone who attended was wearing it.

Many of the garments designed this way have served Cleo's well. The 'two-way fastening coat', for example, in production since the 1970s, remains a strong favourite; its evergreen appeal illustrating how little Cleo has been concerned with transient fashion trends. Over eighty years in business its clothing ranges have been based on enduring values of comfort, luxury and utility, while over the same period, sourcing the range of fabrics and skills to produce them has become increasingly challenging.

KNITWEAR, CRAFT AND HERITAGE

In the 1970s, as exports of ready-to-wear clothing 'became more and more difficult, exports of knitwear continued to increase, but these were not yet, on the whole, at the level of high fashion.'[2] Promising sales of high-volume machine-knits along with the positive profile of Irish knitwear encouraged others to enter the market in the 1970s, producing more fashion-oriented ranges; Michelina Stacpoole and

Cleo's two-way fastening coat has been in production for decades. It was not until the 1980s that Cleo employed for the first time professionals, including Corina Grant (above) to model the clothes alongside friends and family. Here for example, Millie Mantle of Delphi Lodge models the children's wear.

'The Creation' (above right) is modelled with boots and Aran knickerbockers. Its collaborative design process was characteristic of much Cleo manufacture.

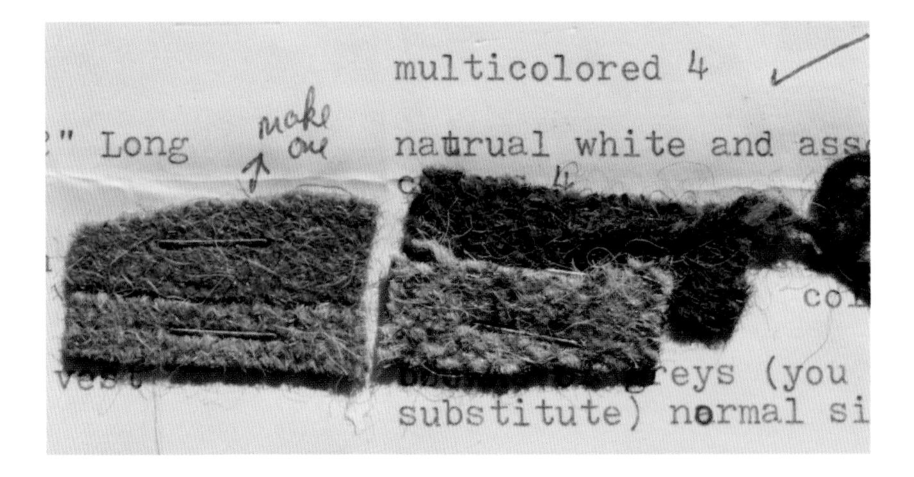

Boiled wool colour samples, from Millars of Clifden, in which 'The Creation' was available.

Cyril Cullen in 1972, Inis Meáin, 1974, Maggie Knits, 1977 and in the 1980s Lyn-Mar, Edel McBride, Glynis Robbins, Eily Doolan, Lainey Keogh and Deirdre Fitzgerald.[3] Later, in the 1980s, Amanda Pratt returned to Ireland to take over knitwear at her family's company Avoca.[4] Cleo were glad to work with several of the new Irish knitwear companies especially as hand knitters were becoming more scarce. These developments in knitwear of course reflected broader changes from handmade, one-off, functional craftwork to a newer emphasis on more design-led 'making'.

This shift took time, facilitated by Ireland's new craft advisory body, established the same year as Crafts Council UK. In 1971 Muriel Gahan and her associates, again set out to help Ireland's craftsmen and women as a voluntary body, the Crafts Council of Ireland, under the chairmanship of Frank Sutton. Among their initiatives was an annual crafts fair, held at the RDS, which Kitty remembers as having the 'spontaneity of a *fleadh cheoil* where the best would come together and exchange ideas.' As its success grew, international buyers were invited and in 1977 the first *Showcase* was held with 34 exhibitors, including Cleo. Today, the event has grown to become a slick commercial enterprise with over 350 exhibitors, not necessarily including Cleo. It is managed by a greatly expanded Crafts Council, described on its website as the 'national design and economic development organisation for the craft industry in Ireland. Its activities are funded by the Department of Jobs, Enterprise, and Innovation via Enterprise Ireland.'

Just as *Showcase* began in 1978, The Country Shop closed the next year. This was the same year controversy erupted over the destruction of Viking heritage at Wood Quay in Dublin. Despite protracted public protest government plans to build offices on the site went ahead. This apparent dismissal of public opinion fuelled an increasing perception that Ireland, as elsewhere, was becoming more corporate and commercial, leading many young people to seek an alternative vision. Already evident in the 1960s, this could by the 1980s, be recognised as an ecologically concerned lifestyle involving 'wholefood shops, re-cycling of bottles and papers, open-air festivals and vegetarianism.'[5] The 1970s and 80s then saw a renewal of the conflict in which craftspeople challenged the values of the commercial world, even as the crafts themselves became more commodified. In 1986 the Crafts Council moved from the RDS to 'HQ' in the Powerscourt Townhouse Centre 'a speciality shopping centre in an elegant Georgian House off Grafton Street'. Here relationships between craft and fine art played out with crafted pieces, more for contemplation than use, presented alongside the sort of functional work once shown in The Country Shop and Cleo – traditional baskets, wooden bowls and ironwork.

Cleo's 'Newgrange' sweater with a pattern based on megalithic stone carving, was designed for 2000 to mark the millennium.

Cleo's handknit sweater design based on the entrance stone at Newgrange.

As established norms and forms in craft were challenged it was soon, according to Tanya Harrod:

> The ways in which craft was written about and consumed which altered most markedly...
>
> Craftspeople are no longer ploughing a quiet furrow in the countryside scraping a living with a clean conscience. They are making big bucks in big cities with articles in colour supplements and answering machines to catch enquiries from Japan'. There was a 'new tone of urgent consumerism and strident populism.'[6]

All of this departure from the past is reflected in a 1990s Crafts Council of Ireland brochure *Training for the 21st century* celebrating the economic significance of knitwear, which 'represented 50% of turnover at Showcase Ireland (£16 million in 1998).' The brochure announces:

> Knit one, purl one
>
> Not anymore. The computer revolution has long since made its mark on the fashion knitwear sector and these days knowledge of software programmes and the capabilities of the high tech systems used by all the major manufacturers is essential for designers.'[7]

Through all these changes Cleo remained focused on the handmade, the one-off and the smaller-scale producer, even as the skill base of the country shifted. To mark the millennium, Kitty designed a sweater based on the entrance stone at Ireland's pre-historic passage tomb, Newgrange, but found it difficult to locate somebody able to translate the knit to a pattern readable by Cleo knitters. The effort however has resulted in a very special garment Kitty hopes might be an Aran for the 21st century.

WEAVING

Into the 1980s Kitty continued to work with a good range of gifted crafts-people. She was able to rely on a rich supply of fabric as surviving skills met the new wave of craft revival weaving, mainly among young women attracted to an alternative lifestyle.[8] Some had trained in handweaving with Lillias Mitchell at the National College of Art & Design, others with Muriel Beckett in Dun Laoghaire College of Art, while some learned from rural weavers, as Nóirín Kennedy did in Donegal. One or two went abroad, like Alice Roden to the Swedish weaver Lily Bohlin, while young weavers from abroad also came to Ireland to set up craft-based enterprises, and lives, here. As early as the 1950s the occasional adventurer had moved to Ireland to weave. Alan and Joy Hemmings, for example moved from

Though Cleo clothing has always connected with Ireland's past, in the 1980s designs based directly on holdings in the National Museum of Ireland were first produced. The pattern for this boiled-wool 'Farmer's Coat' is based on an original in the museum (right).

Frieze coat, made by Thomas Duffy of Claregalway, in the collection of the National Museum of Country Life, Turlough Park, Co Mayo [Museum catalogue F.1967.3]. (Courtesy National Museum of Ireland).

England to set up Donegal Design in a remote part of the county.[9] And about 1985 Beth Moran from Massachussetts began hand-weaving in Clare Island. In the intervening years Helena Ruuth came from Sweden and Bodil Anderson from Denmark, both to work with Kilkenny Design Workshops. Lisbeth Mulcahy also came from Denmark, Cecilia Stephens and Annie Dibble came from England and Junko Okamura from Japan. This revival of interest in weaving led Lillias Mitchell to set up the Irish Guild of Weavers, Spinners and Dyers in 1975.[10] Some of the younger weavers trained in art schools and, asserting a relationship with fine art, might have perceived a distance between what they made and what Cleo sold. Cleo nonetheless saw only the quality of the work and, when suitable, stocked the cloth and rugs of the younger weavers. Alice Roden, for example, remembers Clarissa Webb, who worked with her for two years, selling 'lovely rugs' to Cleo in the late 1980s or early '90s.[11]

At the same period Judith Hoad, who shares many interests with Kitty Joyce in natural and organic living, came to live in Donegal with her family and began her research into local skills and traditions, published in 1987, as *This is Donegal Tweed.*

CLEO CLOTHING AND HERITAGE

Throughout the 20th century mainstream fashion has periodically revisited the past, often in the guise of nostalgia, and in the 1980s Cleo found its styles coincided with a wider romantic vogue, this time self-consciously historicised as 'country-living'. The hugely popular television series, *Brideshead Revisited* (1981), both responded to and encouraged the nostalgic wave. This popular

Anjelica and Ricki Huston, photographed by Arnaud de Rosnay for *Vogue*, c. 1968. Mother and daughter wear Kinsale cloaks made especially for them by Cleo. The Huston family are regarded by Cleo as having been 'great friends to the shop'. Like John Huston's passion for Ireland, their engagement with country life evinces Fiona McCarthy's observation that 'the simple life was never for the simple minded'. (Photograph courtesy Condé Nast Archive, Corbis) [12]

Kinsale cloaks from the Cleo brochure, c. 1970, photographed on the steps of Dublin's Mansion House, by Bill Doyle.

retrospection may have been more about the 'landed' than the land, but it still endorsed the values Cleo had always sought. Handknit and tweed can embody quite separate, even opposing relationships with the land, one patrician the other demotic, a tension Glenn Adamson identifies in the 'pastoral':

> The projection of a rural "golden age" in ... pastoral literature which tacitly claimed the inherent superiority of the gentry, was answered by the (equally pastoral) folk idea of an ideal time of equality, prior to gentry ownership of the land.[13]

Fashion's return to history, combined with a renewed focus on natural fabrics led Kitty to further develop her clothing range based on Ireland's past. Her interest in vernacular clothing had long been supported by staff at the National Museum, whose curators, Dr Anne O'Dowd and the late Mairead Dunlevy, were interested in Cleo's aims and generous with time and expertise. This mutual regard could allow for a very close engagement with historic material. Austin Lendaro, for example, was able to make a direct copy of a 19th century coat, as a model for what Cleo was to sell as 'the Farmer's Coat'. The 'Poet's Coat' and 'General's Coat' were based more indirectly on museum garments. The exchange between Cleo and the museum worked both ways and the folk life curators acquired several pieces from Cleo for their collection, including a handknit jumper (1996) a cloak (2007) and handwoven baskets (2005).

If the role of the National Museum is to preserve and record the past for the future, for Cleo the aim has been to create a living link with Ireland's inheritance. Along with their red wool petticoats, Cleo's Kinsale cloaks are particular examples; both garments originated from at least the 17th century when they were worn throughout Europe, and both remained in use in Ireland for hundreds of years, mainly on the west coast. Less an item of fashionable wear, the Kinsale cloak lasted a lifetime and longer, passed on from generation to generation and serving as a badge of status for the established countrywoman. Until the 1950s the cloaks were still made in Cork and Galway from where Cleo sourced them, but as local orders declined so too did the skills associated with making them. One of the last cloaks they bought for the shop came from Macroom in Cork and this was carefully unpicked by Vera Hennessy to understand its construction and to learn the nuances of how it was made. Once again, Cleo's fostering of the Kinsale cloak illustrates their continuing respect for precisely that which was being abandoned at home, just as it was becoming more appreciated abroad. Cleo nurtured this interest among a metropolitan clientele, sensible to the post-modern romance of the cloak, rather than its pre-modern stigma.

Cleo's clothing range has long evolved in a dialogue between this inheritance and the interests of their clientele. Taking place over decades, refinements incorporate not just Cleo's own vision but responses from customers as well, many of whom are artists, designers, or as Kitty describes it, 'people who are their own people' and those who 'relate to life not to fashion'. Precisely because of Cleo's independence from fashion, their authority was often misunderstood by Irish officialdom, who saw their work and interests as retrograde, failing to get with the times and generally 'out of the loop'.

Much admired in the early 1980s (for instance by buyers for Bloomingdale's, New York) this 'Criss Cross Coat' was heavy and therefore an added challenge to hand knit.

PROMOTING IRELAND ABROAD; AMERICA & BLOOMINGDALES, 1981

Cleo's position in relation to the mainstream was again evident in 1980 when the Irish Trade Board arranged a promotion with Bloomingdale's department store in New York, to bolster trade and exports from Ireland. Cleo thought this a promising initiative, but quickly formed the impression that the Trade Board was none too keen on including them. Government agencies may have seen Cleo as old fashioned and jarring with the image of Ireland they aimed to promote – as young and modern. If so, they may have missed the emerging vogue for the past that was to dominate much 1980s style with Cleo less an irrelevant relic than a harbinger of fashion. Still, Kitty signed up and made arrangements to travel to New York, feeling more tolerated than welcome.

When the Irish trade exhibition was eventually mounted in Bloomingdales in August 1981, a hierarchy among the participants appeared evident to Kitty. Sybil Connolly, understandably, had a prominent position for her prestige goods. Cleo was less prominent, perhaps reflecting an anxiety about how 'modern' Ireland should be represented at such events. Describing an earlier store promotion at Neiman-Marcus, Dallas (1976) the CTT promotions manager, Áine Ryan recalled:

> It wasn't kitschy at all, it was fabulous. CTT didn't want donkeys, red haired children or pigs in the parlour. We were very careful about that sort of thing. But we knew that with Alvin [Colt] in charge, everything would be done with great taste, and it was.[14]

April 24-May 1, 1981 W

New York: The

Perry Ellis' handknit sweaters in earthy four-color mixes, pinwale corduroy pants and Irish knit fezes

Cleo hats were included in Perry Ellis' 1981 collection, shown here in *W* magazine. What Irish eyes may have seen as old-fashioned tassled hats are here styled to emphasise their relevance to contemporary fashion.

Cleo's sense of being somewhat overlooked may have sweetened the success they did achieve in New York. When Kitty and Hanne took time off from Bloomingdales to visit the Metropolitan Museum they were invited to visit the textile conservation department, by Mrs Elizabeth Riley, who despite her name was not in fact Irish. Department staff, all textile professionals, asked to see Cleo samples, and spent several hours in conversation about the Irish clothing and placing orders for their own wardrobes. Kitty went on to show her merchandise to shops on Madison Avenue and was delighted to receive orders 'from two Italian girls in one shop,' and topped off her success with an £800 order from Henri Bendel on 5th Avenue.

In profiling the Bloomingdale's promotion Kitty recalls one prominent US newspaper featured a front-page photograph of Garret Fitzgerald and Ronald Reagan posed in front of Cleo's stand. Using Cleo as a backdrop clearly identified the event as 'Irish', though such theatre may have been seen, by Irish officialdom, as the limit – and perhaps limitation – of what Cleo offered.

Others saw greater potential in Cleo. Before the New York promotion the Trade Board had flown Bloomingdales' buyers to Ireland and ferried them around the country by helicopter. Kitty recalls a representative from CTT coming in to Cleo with four buyers, each of whom became engrossed in choosing garments for themselves, as well as placing orders for Bloomingdales. Indeed she says 'the buyers kept missing other appointments, being too pre-occupied in Cleo.' Among the Bloomingdales delegation to Dublin was the firm's president, Mr Marvin Traub, described as:

> one of the luminaries in the retail sector and known for nurturing young designers such as Ralph Lauren, Donna Karan, Calvin Klein and Tommy Hilfiger, as well as bringing various European designers to the USA such as Yves Saint Laurent, Fendi, Missoni, and Sonia Rykiel.[15]

Mr Traub introduced himself to Kitty saying, 'The women won't leave me alone unless I come here'. Among them was Mrs Jean Shultz, a buyer, now married to Jack Schultz, Vice-President of the store credited with having given Ralph Lauren his first order. Jean Schultz bought a great deal from Cleo, including suits and a 'criss-cross coat' and became a valued customer and promoter of the shop, directing many sales their way.

That the criss-cross coat was not an everyday purchase is confirmed in the correspondence from Carol Brown, who stocked it:

> *5 January 1982*
>
> *Dear Kitty,*
>
> *Believe it or not, we hardly can, we took two orders for The Coat in one day! Wonder if there'll be any more! One customer is waiting for color samples in which it can be made; other is to be my color, and send some matching tweed so she can have a skirt made .. so send maybe 5 yds.. or, if short, 1 ½ yd*
>
> …
>
> *Send me, again, all the dope on The Coat .. price at Dublin, weight, samples, delivery time … etc…*
>
> …
>
> *It would be a GREAT HELP if you included in each sweater a little of the yarn …for mending… and for color reference in ordering.*
>
> *Someone wanted to walk away in my coat.. wonder if I should have let her! It is very comfortable to wear.. even with its weight, it is well balanced.*

And another letter on 8 October 1982:

> *Kitty -*
>
> *Some one tried on my Criss - cross coat + looked wonderful in it. We let her have it. So - it is paid for in this check-*
>
> *I so seldom go out it seemed an ok thing to do- ??? She is Very tall, well set-up, good shoulders - really does it justice!*

The regard Mrs Shultz felt for Cleo was kindled by the same customer care and attention to detail Carmel Snow had admired over twenty years earlier. Beyond supplying clothes, Cleo took pains to help her find a much-desired doll, no longer on the market:

> A male ancestor of Mrs Shultz was from Crilly Co. Donegal. She connected the Crolly Doll with Crilly and dearly wanted one. She asked – but nobody had come up with one. At the time it was stopped production for a few years. Marie

> Murtagh took care of her need – asked John Quinn who worked for Kilcarra yarns [not far from Crilly] to try if there was a dust covered box with a Crolly doll in Donegal. He found one and we were Mrs Shultz's friends for life.

As handmade clothes have become increasingly distinct from manufactured clothing, each purchase, by any of Cleo's customers, will make at least some impact among their own circle, and in Cleo's case many of these were influential. Mrs Shultz, for example, told Kitty she was 'having lunch with Perry Ellis the next week in New York and she would wear our suit'. Perry Ellis, then among New York's most prominent and influential designers must have been impressed, as soon afterwards he visited Cleo, selecting among others, a hat that appeared in the leading fashion industry magazine, *W*.

Kitty recounts as soon as the photograph appeared in *W*:

> Bloomingdale's contacted us and asked why we had not shown them that hat. We had, and their buyer missed it. They sent her over again (from France this time) to see it. It was just the way the designer had fixed it on the head of a model. They wanted to know where Perry Ellis had stood – like they might kiss the floor. You know, we would be getting these people and we would enjoy them, but we wouldn't treat them any differently than anyone else.

The New York trip made a terrific start to the 1980s, a badly needed boost given the disappearance of so many small American-Irish shops. Their demise followed a policy change under the Reagan administration, closing off a concession that allowed small imports into the U.S. tax-free, rendering many shops unviable.

EUROPE

This knock coincided, as Kitty recalls, with Ireland's inflation rate running at 25% and bank interest at 18%. Other markets would have to be found, and with characteristic resolve Kitty started – indeed continued – looking. In 1978, with her eldest son Bryan, aged 16, and her youngest daughter Sarah, she had set out for Amsterdam, knapsacks on their backs containing knitting and weaving samples 'you could be proud to produce'. Hanne Burke was also part of the group. Her native German, and facility with languages, became increasingly essential to Cleo as American trade diminished and communication with Europe expanded.

From the late 1970s ecologically minded consumers in Europe became a focus for Cleo, starting with a 'Natural Fair' in Stuttgart. Advertised as a 'natural goods' event Kitty expected it would be very strict and brought only natural oiled and un-dyed knits. On arrival she found that, in fact, any of her stock would have met the criteria for 'natural'. Outside the fair the flags of participating countries were flying on a nearby hill, and Kitty

Kitty Joyce and Hanne Burke in Germany. Discovering the world, and other cultures, has greatly contributed to Kitty Joyce's enjoyment of Cleo.

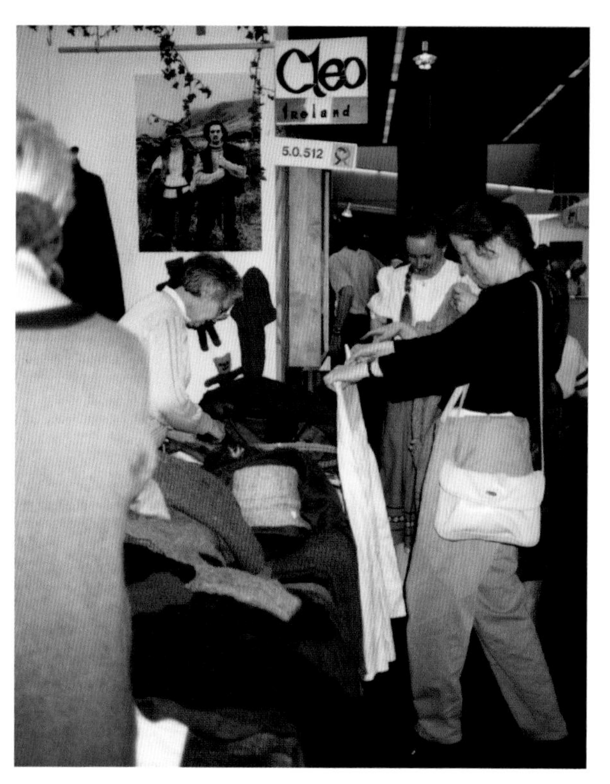

From the late 1970s Cleo began to exhibit in European 'Natural Fair' trade shows. On the first occasion Kitty brought her most 'natural' un-dyed stock only to find it appeared rather monochrome beside other displays. Her solution was to enliven her stand by adorning each sweater with a cut flower. Thereafter she brought her full range of colourful work.

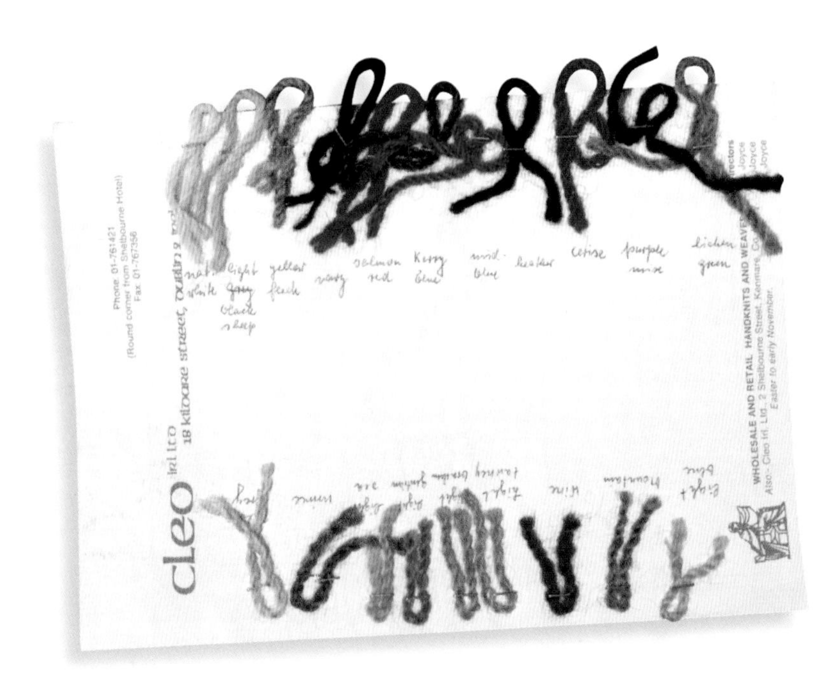

Characteristic care and attention to detail is seen in this Cleo colour card carefully pinned and labelled for ease of reference, by Hanne Burke.

felt quite moved to see the Irish flag, as she was the sole participant from Ireland.

In preparation for their European campaign Cleo sought to establish links through trade board contacts but, perhaps due to mismatches of scale, found the suggestions came to nothing. The trade board mainly targeted bigger operations, but Cleo will nonetheless have benefited from CTT initiatives like 'The Look is Ireland' knitwear campaign focused initially on France, Germany and Italy, and then spun out to their other offices in Belgium, Holland, Japan and USA.'[16] Cleo's strategy instead was to window-shop at night, scouting for places they thought might like their work. Kitty felt they made progress and when 'a magnificent shop in Vienna, all decorated inside with tiles', took her clothes Kitty 'knew the trip was a success'. Many of the orders were for no more than £300, perhaps a figure not worth considering for most companies dealt with by the trade board. However, in Cleo the team headed by Hanne, Marie and Kitty meticulously 'minded' each account, promptly dispatching well-selected goods, so that customers re-ordered and business rolled over. Such small accounts helped sustain Cleo through difficult times, but they were undoubtedly hard work.

JAPAN

In the meantime a further corner of the globe in which interest in Ireland had developed was Japan, and recognising the potential, Ireland's trade board arranged a mission there in the early 1980s, in which Cleo took part. Kitty says their initial introduction to business in Japan had come through Mark Davies, son of Mary and Donald Davies of Enniskerry, whose line of Irish wool dresses had achieved international success. Mark had opened a branch selling Donald Davies clothing in Ginza, Tokyo. Some years earlier Kitty's curiosity about Japan and its craft tradition had been heightened hearing Nicholas Mosse, the Kilkenny potter, talk about his training there. So, to expand her Japanese trip beyond commercial exchange, Kitty travelled with a Japanese friend long resident in Ireland, and

Europeans, particularly Germans, warmed to a 'natural' styling, for example in Cleo's promotional image (left) where the model's dress, pose and basket of woollen skeins suggest an earthy naturalness. In Japan, by contrast, buyers preferred their nature more formally packaged (right).

Photographs from an album, in the Cleo archive, of the early 1980s Irish Trade Board mission to Japan; formal business and cultural exploration.

herself a wonderful craftswoman. They travelled to the countryside together, staying in traditional houses and visiting craftspeople in their workshops. The low wooden table now holding the daily newspapers in Kildare Street was bought from a young woodworker on that trip, thrilled his work was to be used alongside that of Nakashima.

Ireland is seen differently by different cultures and for Kitty each foreign trading relationship requires customised care and sensitivity. For example, Cleo had considerable success selling skeins of wool to nature-loving Europeans, the wool twists becoming a feature in promotions and in the shop. The skeins had long been popular even among Irish women, who found it increasingly difficult to buy local wool suitable for hand-knitting and regarded Cleo as their best source. But, when filling an order for wool from Japan she shipped some of these bulky rustic hanks to Yokahama, her client immediately sent back a photograph of a contrasting tidy 50g ball of wool:

> *In Japan they sell the woolen yarns in this style. Do you have this kind of tape? It's very important to decorate the goods. They must be good-looking. When I have the Aran's woolen yarns in this style, I will be able to sell more in Japan (March 2nd 1977)*

Helen Joyce, Kitty and Tom's middle daughter, in Cleo, Kenmare, which opened in 1985. Cleo later experimented with outlets in different locations. For example, in 1990 Kitty opened in Enniskerry, Co Wicklow, and franchised an outlet in Eton, England. Neither, however, survived very long.

CLEO, KENMARE

Cleo's strategy of nurturing interest in their knitwear around the globe served them well right up to the mid 1980s, even while others suffered economic downturns.

In Putney, Vermont, where (like Cleo's) Carol Brown's clientele ranged across a spectrum from a wealthy elite to the bohemian, the impact of the 1980s worldwide recession was more severe. Therefore the healthy sales reported by Cleo came as a surprise, 'We hear from Avoca that business is very good .. and you write the same. Very interesting.. odd too.. over here the story is mostly QUITE the opposite. With us, it is almost at the tragic point.' (11 May 1981)

Cleo, however, eventually felt the recession and in addressing how to counter its effects it struck Kitty, while attending a Joyce niece's wedding in Ashford Castle, that rural tourism had been less badly hit than in Dublin. She considered opening a new Cleo, first in Cong, Co Mayo, not only home to the five star hotel but also the central location for *The Quiet Man* (1952), but then chose Kenmare, Co Kerry, a town she finds 'full of energy'. In 1985 Cleo opened at No 2 Shelbourne Street, close to the highly acclaimed Park Hotel, and their success in the town has been

in great part due to location, but also to Kitty's middle daughter, Helen, moving to Kerry to run it. 'Kenmare saved Dublin' is how Kitty puts it, remembering how business 'dipped' in Dublin in the 1980s.

MAIL ORDER AND SHOPPING GUIDES

Opening in Kerry, travelling to Europe, the United States and Japan have all served Cleo well, and indeed like any good business professional Kitty appreciates the need to seek out and nurture in person trading relationships, however distant. On many occasions however the world discovers her. One standout instance was that of a mighty US mail-order company, J. Peterman, whose strap line declares: 'Traveling the World to find uncommonly good stuff'. Apart from commercial success, the J. Peterman Company became celebrated in the mid-1990s in a character on the hit television comedy *Seinfeld*. Like the fictional Mr J. Peterman, the real-life counterpart based his brand on esoteric, romantic, vaguely nostalgic, high-quality garments sourced throughout the globe. Described in *The New York Times*, Sunday Magazine as a 'merchant poet';[17] he observed of his eponymous firm 'When you buy from Peterman you are not buying a piece of fabric, you are travelling the world with me'.

'Merchant poet' might equally well describe Kitty Joyce; in any case her range and Ireland's reputation reached a new and wider audience through J. Peterman. An arresting image in the Cleo archive is Richard Avedon's portrait of Steven Spielberg in a handknit sweater, from Cleo, as Kitty recounts, that was ordered from the J. Peterman catalogue. Richard Avedon had visited Ireland with Carmel Snow in 1953 and stayed in the Shelbourne Hotel. He credits the Harper's Bazaar editor with having greatly influenced his work: quoted on the jacket of her biography he declares 'Carmel Snow taught me everything I know'.[18]

Peterman was just one of many influential and discriminating tastemakers outside Ireland to celebrate their discovery of Cleo. Again and again, the archive shows that the Kildare Street shop won endorsement abroad from distinguished magazines covering Ireland's fashion. Cleo also features in specialist guides published in Europe, Japan and America, including Suzy Gershman's bible of the local, independent and artisan, *Born to Shop*. Over 26 years a multi-million selling guide, its 1991 edition encouraged visitors, under 'Dublin/Sweaters', to turn the corner by The Shelbourne Hotel and find:

> *CLEO:*
> *As far as we are concerned, Cleo's is the best shop in Ireland. It's not big, it doesn't sell a lot of things, and it's not glitzy. All it has is handknit sweaters and tweeds made into women's ready-to-wear. Both are of the highest quality and combine the best in fashion looks with a current fashion sense to perfect the rich country look. This means there are about six different skirt styles, including a mini. You can also get a Kinsale cloak or a tweed coat dress; in spring they sell linen. But we digress from our main subject: sweaters. The back parlor of this tiny town-house space is filled with sweaters, most in solid heathery, tweedy, or hand-dyed colors, and all in*

Opposite: *Steven Spielberg, director, Los Angeles, February 11, 1994*
Photograph by Richard Avedon

> *the $125 - $150 range. There are some intricate knits of the Kaffe Fassett type in the $500 price range, but just a few. There's a wide range of styles in sweaters, and some sweater coats. Everything is Irish but very wearable in a suburban American way.*[19]

SELLING THE LOOK: A NEW CATALOGUE

Gershman's admiring, compact pen-picture flagged just the qualities in Cleo clothes that would assimilate them to a contemporary taste – modern and practical yet individual and traditional. Cleo itself was able to meet this renewed appreciation with a wholly new catalogue, for the first time presenting a rounded vision of their clothes in large-scale international-quality images. A production of this quality was beyond Cleo's own resources, and here they were given the support they needed from CTT. This was largely achieved through Rose Mary Craig who Kitty considers fully understood Cleo's vision and oversaw a very generous grant towards the catalogue's cost, of a sum matched by Cleo. A substantial undertaking, this new brochure was carefully planned and carried through with high production values at every stage. Designed by Kitty, along with Catherine Tobin, they drew up a model book, rather like a film storyboard. Kitty had a clear sense of the tone the images should convey, and independent as ever, the narratives she wanted to suggest were not the typical tropes of fashion. She envisaged 'an uncle meeting a favourite niece, not sex' and to show the Poet's Coat she wanted to avoid any sense of a 'craw-thumping preacher' and capture instead 'a melancholic poet with T.B.'

The catalogue was set in Delphi, Co Mayo close to where *The Field* was shot in 1990. This time the fashion shoot was styled by Elizabeth Clare, whose work with Cleo clothes (in Irish magazine fashion shoots) had greatly impressed Kitty. Photography was by Mike Bunn who Kitty recalls enjoyed working with Cleo clothes because they stood up to the surroundings. His images superbly married Cleo fabrics and landscape to reflect the rich harmonies between them.

The evocative images in the brochure suggest strong independent figures comfortably, if moodily, at home in the wilds. The women, in jackets, waistcoats and trousers, now with confident direct gazes, seem generations away from some of the more endearing 'girls' of the first colour catalogue of not two decades earlier. If this all reflects not just a changing Ireland but advances for women everywhere, now more self-assured and liberated, it is interesting that Cleo's clothes themselves have hardly changed at all.

Although the clothing range has been modified in subtle ways over the decades the circumstances in which Cleo operates have changed dramatically, even since moving to Kildare Street, not to mention Molesworth Street or South Anne Street. Since opening in Kildare Street in the 1970s so much has changed in Irish clothing, craft and culture: the visit of Pope John Paul II (1979) is seen by many, in retrospect, as the grand finale of a familiar Ireland, the election of Mary Robinson (1990) as the promise of a new culture, although the same year Jim Sheridan's film *The Field* projected a nostalgia, even for a tortured past. In 2004 the

A Cleo 'Caped Coat' illustrated in the J. Peterman catalogue.
The caption read:

'As Irish as Black Pudding

Dublin

A While back.

Heading North on Kildare.

Spot a shop just before Nassau Street called Cleo.

Raw Irish Wool Sweaters that still had the oil in them.

Authentic fisherman pants and vests.

I had found my home away from home.

We did so much business over the years, Kitty, the owner, wanted to give me something as a "token of her gratitude."

I began to protest until I saw the Marvellous Herringbone 'Caped Coat' (No 2808) she had in her Hands. Solid weight (530/560 gms/mtr).

The original resides in my closet

When I'm not wearing it.

We had the fabric perfectly duplicted in Donegal.'

Model, Corina Grant, wears the 'General's Coat', Diarmuid Boyd the 'Caped Coat'.

purchase by Irishmen of Claridge's hotel in London confirmed a changed Ireland, and the arrival of the International Monetary Fund in Dublin (2011) can only be seen as the decisive end of an era.

Over the same period the direction taken in the world of crafts, in Ireland and well beyond, are almost as dramatic, and encapsulated by Martina Margetts in a rich analysis of forty years of the crafts in the United Kingdom:

> In the 1970s …the traditions of hand-made craft remained – domestic thrown tableware, silver spoons, elegant furniture – supported by guild societies and rural craft associations and apprenticeships but by the end of the decade the word 'post-modern' fitted the crafts very well:
>
> … By the 1980s the crafts were now being contextualised, theorised or subjected to critical review…
>
> … The design and craft worlds collaborated in ushering in a more ecologically conscious decade, a reaction to perceived excesses past. The emphasis on sustainability and on recycling brought with it a new aesthetic and a wish to make things more affordable but the self-reliant dignity and pleasure of craftsmanship and labour is today played out in much more ambiguous times. We cannot continue to ignore the realities of repressive production, in India and China for example. There craftwork of beauty and utility is produced for Western consumption on unfair terms and – worse still – commodities of no aesthetic merit or traditions of excellent making are churned out on a vast scale so that the identity of place with maker, technique and material is perverted. …
>
> Today practitioners, or now simply artists, are exploring narratives of the uncanny, the dematerialised, the virtual, more speculative in form material process and purpose than ever before. It may not matter that many argue there is no such thing as a crafts world, with craft histories and disciplines blurred as new technologies and new collaborative practices afford new possibilities and traditional materialities and locations of craft objects are disregarded.
>
> The affirmative view seems to be that no boundaries are surely best for the future dynamic health of crafts. Last year's events – A History of the World in 100 Objects and The Hare with Amber Eyes – together arguably show us that objects are the means by which we identify ourselves and our cultures.[20]

Through all these reconfigurations of the contexts in which crafts are presented Cleo has continued to engage with crafts both locally and across the globe in a relationship which is consequently nuanced. Perhaps Cleo's strength has been, in the absence of any defining label, hierarchy or jurisdiction, to retain their own conviction about what they do. Relishing the complex nature of what they sell as not quite fashion, craft, art, or design but work that touches 'people's lives in unexpected ways.'[21]

Through all the changes Cleo, or more precisely Kitty, 'has been different', according to Rose Mary Craig of CTT, 'she stands alone, like a continent, offering her work to anyone who would like it.' Kitty's steadfastness to clothing as a crafted local product appears to have gained her sustained custom from visitors, while

An image from Cleo's brochure (c.1993), by far its most accomplished and succesful to date. A fully rounded picture of the clothes and their context was realised through a team effort: designed by Kitty Joyce and Catherine Tobin, styled by Elizabeth Clare and photographed by Mike Bunn on location in Delphi, Co. Mayo, over a wet St. Patrick's weekend. Persevering despite the weather, Bunn judged that wool and tweed could stand up to conditions that would 'kill other fabrics'. Models credited in catalogue as : Tijam and Trevor.

distancing her from local custom. Perhaps Cleo in Kildare Street, home of the National Library and National Museum, represents something of the paradox explored by Declan Kiberd in his analysis of the literature of modern Ireland:

> Of persons who seem at once fixated on the past and supremely indifferent to it. Their surroundings seem decontextualized, because they represent a geography which has been deprived of a history. The historian Louis Cullen has spoken of "the general poverty of tradition in Ireland", which is why the people view their country "uncertainly and apologetically". Another scholar noting the indifference of country folk to local antiquities, likens them to people condemned to live without a key in a superbly coded environment.[22]

Endnotes

1 McCrum, Elizabeth (1997) *Fabric & Form*, Belfast, Ulster Museum, pp. 47-53.

2 Ibid. p. 48.

3 Ibid. pp. 74-79.

4 Carey, Anna (2011) 'Dream Weavers' in *Trinity Today*, Issue 16, pp. 32-33.

5 Harrod, Tanya (1999) *The Crafts in Britain in the 20th Century*, New Haven and London, Yale, p. 459.

6 Ibid. p. 411.

7 Crafts Council of Ireland brochure, '*Training for the 21st century*', text by Róisín Ingle, NIVAL.

8 In 1977 The Crafts Council of Ireland held an exhibition 'Centuries of Wool' in Bank of Ireland Exhibition Centre, Baggot Street (16 Sept – 8 Oct) research for which became the basis of E.F. Sutton's 1980 book. In NIVAL a photocopy of the Baggot Street brochure records the following mills were represented by examples of typical tweeds:

Millars Connemara Tweeds Ltd, Clifden
John Hanly & Son Ltd, Barryartella Mills, Nenagh
Robert Eadie & Sons Ltd, Kerry Woollen Mills, Beaufort
Providence Woollen Mills, Foxford
Hill & Sons Ltd, Lucan
McNutt Handweaving Co. Ltd, Downings
Magee & Co. Ltd, Donegal
Dripsey Woollen Mills Ltd, Dripsey
Cushendale Mills, Graiguenamanagh

9. Hemmings, Alan (2013) *The Friendship of Total Strangers*, Louis Hemmings, louis@samovarbooks.com

10 See EF Sutton (1980) *Weaving: The Irish Inheritance*, Dublin, Gilbert Dalton, pp 63–64.

Mitchell, Lillias (1972) *The Wonderful Work of the Weaver*, Dublin, John Augustine.

Mitchell, Lillias (1986) *Irish Weaving: discoveries and personal experiences*, Dundalk, Dundalgan Press. www.weavers.ie

Hoad, Judith (1987) *This is Donegal Tweed*, Donegal, Shoestring Publications.

11 O'Kelly, Hilary (24 January 2013) email correspondence with Alice Roden.

12 Fiona McCarthy, quoted in Glenn Adamson *Thinking Through Craft*, Oxford, New York, Berg, p. 106.

13 Adamson, Glenn (2007) *Thinking Through Craft*, Oxford, New York, Berg, p. 107.

14 Moran, Anna (2011) 'Tradition in the Service of Modernity' in Linda King and Elaine Sisson, *Ireland, Design and Visual Culture: Negotiating Modernity, 1922–1992*, Cork, Cork University Press, p. 206.

15 Marvin Traub: Executive Profile & Biography, investing.businessweek.com, accessed 28 August 2012.

16 O'Kelly, Hilary (16 September 2010) in conversation with Rose Mary Craig, Enniskerry.

17 Peterman, John (2000) *Peterman Rides Again*, New Jersey, Prentice Hall Press, p. 84.

18 Rowlands, Penelope (2005) *A Dash of Daring*, New York, Atria Books.

19 Gershman, Suzy (1991) *Born to Shop*, New York, Bantam Books, pp. 330–3.

20 Margetts, Martina (2011) 'From Leach to Etsy', catalogue essay for 'Collect' 2011 available on Crafts Council UK website 'We Are 40' www.craftscouncil.org.uk/about-us/leach-to-etsy/files/mobile/index.html#1

21 Harrod, Tanya op.cit. p. 463.

22 Kiberd, Declan (1995) *Inventing Ireland*, London, Jonathan Cape, pp. 539–540.

CLEO – LOOKING BACK AND FORWARD

The international fashion system today is built around a fixed timetable of constant change that conjures an illusion of responsiveness to seasons and years, in pursuit of the elusive 'now'. By contrast, Cleo clothing has through almost eighty years, sought not manufactured transience but rootedness and connection, with people, tradition and place. Both merchandise and business relate more to rhythms of life and nature than to the contrived 'seasons' of the fashion calendar. Throughout, Cleo's essence has been the nurturing of relationships, between makers and materials, garments and promotion, business and customers, country and city.

Continuity, community, unity of life – these have been the hallmarks of a vision that has sustained Cleo in a stance independent from the wider sweep of commercial, even official, policy in Ireland. Against a tendency to seek modernity through the import of technology, capital and culture, Cleo recognised the modernity inherent in the traditional and rural. The opposition of city and country so prevalent in popular culture is not borne out in the experience of many, including Kitty Joyce. As the daughter of two country people who made their livelihoods in the city, Kitty herself became a businesswoman married to a man who farms. And in Cleo, Kitty and her mother created a space supporting the view that 'equating the country with man in nature and the city with man in society is simply wrong, a false dichotomy'. [1]

In Cleo the cloth and clothing are both a way of living and a business. For Kitty Joyce, who always wears the clothes she sells, the shop is part of her wider vision and beliefs, valuing people, nature and creativity over systems, commodities and commercialization. Cleo is as much about how to be as about what to buy. Concerning her clientele Kitty retains a business-like discretion, as she does about suppliers. 'Cleo never built its reputation on the back of its customers and it's not needing to now'. She has found, in any case, that anyone drawn to the shop on some notion of celebrity association never 'gets' what Cleo is about. As she says, Cleo customers are 'their own people', suggesting perhaps that they stand somewhat aside from dominant fashion trends, being individually stylish and personally confident.

Kitty's discretion notwithstanding, her customers contacted through other avenues have been happy to discuss Cleo; for many it encapsulates the very qualities they admire about the country. One, Madame Catherine Michel, aware that she 'may sound romantic' says that 'Cleo is what Ireland means to me. It is eternal'.[2] A world-renowned harpist, Mme Michel first came to Ireland in the 1960s to join the National Concert Orchestra. In the 1980s she returned to France as solo harpist at the Paris National Orchestra and continues to tour the world with her composer husband, Michel Legrand. For Cleo knitting she maintains a special regard. Experience has shown her that shopping for clothes abroad is not always a success; so often garments bought on her travels are difficult to integrate into her wardrobe on her return home. But Cleo knitting 'always looks well, you will have it forever; it will forever be elegant, forever special. It is out of time – *intemporal*'. On return trips to Ireland she has a '*chemin de croix*' [Stations of the Cross] on which Cleo is an important stop. She contrasts Cleo clothes with ubiquitous superficial fashions, and garments that offer initial gratification but loose body and form after one or two washes. Her grandmother, a dressmaker who taught her the value of quality in fabric, would test a material by feel, and, if not up to standard, dismiss it as a sponge or a floor cloth. Mme Michel's upbringing taught her that quality is vital to all creativity. Quality in anything, she says, is like quality in music; 'only achieved through practice, investment and honesty.'

Such an admiring, even idealised, image of Ireland echoes that of John Huston, in valuing a place felt to be more true and real, encapsulated in Cleo in hand crafted wool. But of course, balancing such abstraction, more physical, practical qualities also characterise Cleo knitwear. The natural warmth it offers – warmth so unlike that of central heating or synthetic fabrics – may be just as much the deciding factor for Cleo customers as its handcraft value. For all its exceptional qualities of material and making the clothing is well priced and easily comparable to designer wear sold along Grafton Street. Indeed in any department store it is possible to find many similarly priced, if not more expensive, sweaters offered by major international brands. Occasionally these are even marketed through a notional association with Ireland; sweaters called 'Donegal' for example, with no connection to Ireland beyond this styling tag. To the international market for 'country wear' such an evocation of Irish rurality may be appealing. But at home Cleo's distinctive handmade style may appear for some all too local and familiar.

Wool and linen are indeed deeply rooted in Irish culture, traded internationally for centuries, and Cleo has been exceptional in sustaining this tradition of quality handmade produce into the 21st century. Similarly their approach to business carried into the modern era an older more personalised way of trading. The enterprise built up by Kit Ryan was rooted in the shopping culture of 19th and early 20th century rural Ireland.[3] Then retail businesses were mostly run by families whose values and character established their personal and trading standing in the community, measured by such qualities as value, honesty, reliability and generosity. More personally identified with their businesses, many traders did not simply retail products but balanced relationships of family, community, customers and suppliers. They knew each customer, their needs, preferences and means and played a part in balancing them, each account known and nurtured. This culture, carried to Dublin by Kit Ryan, later met the modernising impetus of T.K. Whittaker, Bill Walsh and the Kilkenny Design Workshops – and was adapted to serve Dorothy Jeakins in Hollywood or Lady Birley in Sussex with the same attention and tact a rural shopkeeper would bring to a valued customer in the next town. Most shops, in Ireland, carried the family name above the door but in 1936 Kit Ryan's instinct and economic savvy saw merit in adopting the name Cleo in South Anne Street, declaring a more modern vision while retaining an older culture of business. At each step, Cleo has balanced a recognition of modern market forces with the expression of its own ethos, ideas and direction.

Though these handmade clothes and fabrics may suggest a resistance to change, Cleo has in fact always worked with change, from its business context to its markets and clientele, while perceptions of natural materials themselves have constantly varied. Appreciation for Cleo's clothes is affected not just by customers' own experience, but by the inherited reputation of Irish wools and linens. The prestige of these fabrics has stemmed in part from their inherent tactile qualities but also – as noted by Lou Taylor in her exploration of fabric hierarchies – partly from their expense and the care required in maintaining them.[4] But though esteemed, their fashionability is not fixed, being recast over time, as 'real' in an age of synthetics, as stable in an age of conflict or change, and more recently as ecological in an age of sustainability anxiety.

The general status of hand knitting has been even less certain. For many it lacks sufficient 'distinction' to achieve high status, challenged by its ubiquity, utility, cosiness, sturdiness and capacity to be unravelled and re-made. In Ireland the legacies of nationalism, self-sufficiency and cultural politics can intrude even on the wearing of such distinctive garments, with for some the craft appearing to wear the person, rather than the person wearing the craft. But the world is changing and qualities once regarded with misgivings are now being recast as strengths. Conspicuous consumption has lost some of its gloss and mindless waste is disparaged. Knowing what you are buying, where it was sourced and who made it is increasingly a consideration in consumer choice.

The characteristics that distinguish Cleo's wear – natural, textured, rural, homely, earthy and pre-industrial – have long struck a chord with visitors to Ireland. While the shop may be off the popular tourist route, Cleo's archive records its long-standing appeal, for instance to visiting journalists, and indicates a separate network of travel wisdom operating outside the official tourism 'loop'. In international magazine coverage of quality Irish travel, craft and fashion, from North America to Europe and Asia, Cleo is almost invariably included.

In Irish coverage this is less the case. Here, a small, if distinguished roster of names is regularly invoked to represent the country's fashion and textiles; Sybil Connolly, Irene Gilbert, Néillí Mulcahy, John Rocha and Lainey Keogh, all of whom have indeed been impressive ambassadors for Ireland and Irish cloth and clothing. In Irish craft and design it is The Country Shop, the Crafts Council and Kilkenny Design Workshops that constitute the 20th century canon of influence. And for clothes retailing most attention has understandably been focused on the great department stores of Clerys, Switzers, Brown Thomas and Arnotts. Through all this time (pre-dating Kilkenny Design and outliving Switzers) Cleo has been a quiet sustained presence, smaller but as significant as any other enterprise in holding up Ireland's reputation for quality wool and linen and sustaining the narrative of Ireland as a place more closely connected to the natural, the sociable and the human scale.

That narrative (and traditional Irish textile production) has increasingly had to contend with modern realities of influence, competition and even regulation from the United States and from Europe. What were originally foundational textile enterprises, set up in the wake of the Famine and in early independent

Ireland to alleviate poverty and nurture home industry, now face very different circumstances, from economic background to national self-image. Kennedy & McSharry, trading as 'Dublin's oldest and finest men's outfitters' since 1890, in 2012 moved to smaller premises, while despite trading well, The Woollen Mills, established in 1888, closed its doors in the same year.

> Valerie Roche, granddaughter of the founder, Valentine Roche, spoke of the bureaucratic burden – 'half our time is spent filling in forms' – and how it weighs on small businesses and family firms. Ms Roche expressed concern at the government approach to job creation; that it's all 'Dell, Google, pharmaceuticals – they think they're sorting the problem with the multinationals, but 80 per cent of people are, or used to be, employed in small business'. In recent years Valerie Roche points to a huge revival in the market trade and growth in small businesses run by women. 'Probably 25 per cent of our wholesale accounts are new accounts started in the last two or three years and 90 per cent of them are women'. [5]

Women, often assumed to have had little role in commercial Ireland, were also at the helm of many enterprises and initiatives considered here. Cleo, The Country Shop, Slynes, Cathcarts and the NAIDA showcase in Stephen's Green, were all run by women, some married, some single, some widowed. That they could prosper independently contests, at least in part, the inherited picture of the restriction of women in early independent Ireland.

In Cleo a third generation of women is now in place. Kitty Joyce, in her early 80s, has just retired to pursue new adventures including Tai Chi. In Kenmare, Helen Joyce is expanding the Cleo enterprise to incorporate a gallery and exhibition space while in Dublin, Sarah Joyce is building on the work of her mother and grandmother in sourcing quality handmade cloth and clothing to offer the world from Kildare Street. Cleo is now poised, its original ethos intact, to meet the new circumstances of the 21st century as independent trading, small-scale production, sustainable development, eco-tourism and buying less to last longer, are set to become a new norm. Over three generations and three quarters of a century Cleo has balanced change and continuity, and nurtured textile traditions through a market place evolving from shop counter to internet, from regional to global, and from small-scale manufacture to assembly-line production. Industrial production has of course been essential for Irish economic progress as well as for consumer choice, but a national economy needs to be dynamic and robust, it needs variety, and government must make space, not only for multi-nationals, but also for quality niche products. Cleo is evidence that, in the right hands, it can thrive.

Endnotes

1 Adamson, Glenn (2007) *Thinking Through Craft*, Oxford, Berg, p.107.

2 O'Kelly, Hilary (20 August 2010) Interview with Mme. Catherine Michel, The Conrad Hotel, Dublin,

with many thanks to Geraldine O'Doherty for this introduction and for kindly arranging our meeting.

3 According to anthropologist Conrad Arensberg, Ireland in 1937 was better supplied with shops than any other comparable European nation. Most shops carried the family name above the door and constituted 'a seat of familistic identification'.

Arensberg, Conrad (1937) *The Irish Countryman*, New York, Macmillan, p. 139.

4 Taylor, Lou (2003) 'The Hierarchy of Fashion Fabrics' in Schoeser, Mary and Christine Boydell, *Disentangling Textiles*, London, Middlesex University Press.

5 O'Halloran, Marie (16 June 2012) *The Irish Times* ' Joyce's 'Irish Homespuns' shop to close'.

SELECT BIBLIOGRAPHY

ADAMSON, GLENN (2007) *Thinking Through Craft*, Oxford, New York, Berg.

ARENSBERG, CONRAD (1937) *The Irish Countryman*, New York, Macmillan.

BRADY, J AND ANNGRET SIMMS (2001) *Dublin Through Space & Time*, Dublin, Four Courts Press.

BURMAN, BARBARA (1999) *The Culture of Sewing: Gender, Consumption and Home Dressmaking*, Oxford, Berg.

CAFFREY, PAUL (1998) 'The Scandinavian Ideal: a model for design in Ireland', *Scandinavian Journal of Design History*, Denmark.

CAFFREY, PAUL (2009) 'Primary Text, Commentary' in *The Journal of Modern Craft*, Volume 2 – Issue 3, pp 325-330, Oxford, Berg.

CAREY, ANNA (2011) 'Dream Weavers' in *Trinity Today*, issue 16 October p 32-33, Dublin.

CLERY, ELIZABETH (2003) *Néilli Mulcahy Couturiére 1951 – 1969*, unpublished MA thesis, National College of Art & Design.

COSTELLO, PETER & T. FARMAR (1992) *The Very Heart of The City, The story of Denis Guiney and Clery's Dublin*, Dublin, A&A Farmar.

COSTELLO, PETER, (2008) *Denis Guiney*, Dublin, University College Dubin Press.

DALY, MARY E. (1992) *Industrial Development and Irish National Identity, 1922-1939*, Dublin, Gill And Macmillen.

DALY GOGGIN, MARY AND BETH FOWKES TOBIN, *Women and the Material Culture of Needlework and Textiles, 1750 – 1950*, Farnham, Ashgate.

DE LA HAYE, AMY and V. MENDES (1999) *Twentieth Century Fashion*, London, Thames & Hudson

Design In Ireland (1962) Published by *Córas Tráchtála*

DOYLE, ROSE (2004) *Trade Names: traditional traders and shopkeepers of Dublin*, Dublin, New Island.

DRURY, CLARE (2006) *Hand Knitting rural Ireland c.1940- 1960*, unpublished BA thesis, National College of Art & Design.

DUNLEVY, MAIREAD (1989) *Dress In Ireland*, London, Batsford.

FARMAR, TONY (1995) *Ordinary Lives; The private lives of three generations of Ireland's professional classes.* Dublin, A&A Farmar.

FERRITER, DIARMAID (2004) *The Transformation of Ireland 1900 – 2000*, London, Profile Books.

GAUNTLETT, DAVID (2011) *Making is Connecting*, Cambridge, Polity.

GERSHMAN, SUZY (1991) *Born to Shop*, England, Scotland, and Ireland. New York, N.Y., Bantam Books.

GRIFFIN, RUTH (2007) *The Lost History of South William Street*, unpublished MA theis, London College of Fashion.

HAVERTY, ANNE (1995) *Elegant Times; A Dublin Story*, Dublin, Sonas.

HARROD, TANYA (1999) *The Crafts in Britain in the 20th Century*, New Haven; London, Yale University Press.

HELLAND, JANICE (2007) *British and Irish Home Arts and Industries 1880- 1914*, Dublin, Irish Academic Press.

HEMMINGS, ALAN (2013) *The Friendliness of Total Strangers: A Donegal Adventure*, Louis Hemmings, louishemmings@samovarbooks.com.

HEMMINGS, JESSICA (2012) *The Textiles Reader*, Oxford, Berg.

HOAD, JUDITH (1987) *This Is Donegal Tweed*, Inver, Co. Donegal, Shoestring.

HOPKINS, ARLENE (2007) *Murphy Sheehy: The biggest little treasure trove*, unpublished BA thesis, National College of Art & Design.

KENNEDY, B.P. AND R. GILLESPIE (1994) *Ireland Art into History*, Dublin, Town House.

KIBERD, DECLAN (1995) *Inventing Ireland, The Literature of Modern Ireland*, London, Jonathan Cape.

KING, LINDA AND ELAINE SISSON ed.s (2011) *Ireland, Design and Visual Culture: Negotiating Modernity, 1922–1992*, Cork, Cork University Press.

MAHON, BRID (2000) *Rich and Rare; The Story of Irish Dress*, Cork; Dublin, Mercier Press.

MC CRUM, ELIZABETH (1997) *Fabric & Form; Irish Fashion since 1950*, Belfast, Ulster Museum.

MCQUILLAN, DEIRDRE (1993) *The Aran Sweater*, Belfast, Appletree.

MITCHELL, LILLIAS (1972) *The Wonderful Work of The Weaver*, Dublin, John Augustine.

MITCHELL, LILLIAS (1978) *Irish Spinning, Weaving and Dying; An Anthology from original documents*, Dundalk, Dundalgan Press.

MITCHELL, LILLIAS (1986) *Irish Weaving: Discoveries And Personal Experience*, Dundalk, Dundalgan Press.

MITCHELL, GERALDINE (1997) *Deeds Not Words; The Life and Work of Muriel Gahan, Champion of Rural women and Craftworkers*, Dublin, Town House.

NESBITT, RONALD (1993) *AT Arnotts of Dublin*, Dublin, A&A Farmar.

O'BRIEN, KATE (1984), *Without My Cloak*, London, Virago (First published, 1931, London, William Heinemann.)

O'BYRNE, ROBERT (2000) *After a Fashion, A History of The Irish Fashion Industry*, Dublin, Town House.

O'DOWD, ANNE (1990) *Common Clothes & Clothing 1860-1930*, Dublin, National Museum of Ireland.

O'KELLY, HILARY (1992) 'Reconstructing Irishness' in *Chic Thrills* eds Ash, Juliet and Elizabeth Wilson, London, Pandora.

PETERMAN, JOHN (2000) *Peterman Rides Again, Adventures Continue with the real "J Peterman" through Life & the Catalogue Business*, NJ, Prentice Hall Press.

POTTERTON, HOMAN (2001) *Rathcormick, A Childhood Recalled*, Dublin, New Island Books.

RAINS, STEPHANIE (2010) *Commodity Culture & Socail Class in Dublin*, Dublin, Irish Academic Press.

ROWLANDS, PENELOPE (2005) *A Dash of Daring, Carmel Snow and her life in Fashion, Art and Letters*, New York, Atria Books.

RYAN, LOUISE (1998) 'Constructing "Irishwoman": Modern girls and comely maidens' in *Irish Studies Review* Vol. 6, Issue 3.

RYAN, VERA (2003) *Movers & Shapers; Irish Art Since 1960* Cork, The Collins Press.

RYAN, VERA (2006) *Movers & Shapers; Irish Visual Art 1940-2006*, Cork, The Collins Press.

RYAN, VERA (2010) *Movers & Shapers 3; Converstaions in The Irish art World*, Cork, Galley Head Press.

SAYRES NUTTALL, MEGHAN (2001) 'Conversations in Donegal: Mary McNeillis and Con O'Gara' *New Hibenia Review* 5.3 pp 9-21, Dublin, Irish Publication Agency.

SENNETT, RICHARD and C. CALHOUN (2007) *Practicing Culture*, London, New York, Routledge.

SENNETT, RICHARD (2008) *The Craftsman*, London, Allen Lane.

SCOTT, YVONNE (2005) *The West as Metaphor*, Dublin, RHA.

SHERIDAN, JOHN D. (1958, May), 'Bespoke Clothing' *Creation*, Dublin, Fleet Publications.

THACKERA, JOHN (2005) *In The Bubble: Designing In A Complex World*, Cambridge, Mass. And London, MIT Press.

TOBIN, FERGAL, (1984) *The Best of Decades: Ireland in the 1960s*, Dublin, Gill & Macmillan.

TURNEY, JOANNE (2009) *The Culture of Knitting*, Oxford, Berg.

TURPIN, JOHN (1996) 'The Irsh Design Reform Movement of the 1960s' in *Design Issues,* Volume 3, No.1, MIT Press.

USHER, ROBIN (2008) *Dawson, Molesworth & Kildare Strrets D2*, Dublin, Dublin Civic Trust.

NEWSPAPER ARTICLES

MC CUTCHEON, MARY, 08.12.1971, *The Irish Independent,* Independent Woman.

'Irish Hand Knitting in Trouble' 29.05.69, *The Irish Press* 1969

'Irish Craftwork on Exhibition; 100 Items selected', 12.08.70, *The Irish Times*,

ONLINE SOURCES

Beattie, Seán, *Donegal Annual 2009* 'Cottage Industries: Arts and Crafts in Donegal 1810 – 1920' www.historyofdonegal.com/DonegalAnnual09_seans.pdf

Dail Debates, debates.oireachtas.ie

Larry David, Seinfld and J. Peterman – You Tube www.youtube.com/watch?v=_JYXQabSCcA

INDEX